THINK TANK
THE STORY OF THE ADAM SMITH INSTITUTE
MADSEN PIRIE

\B^b\

Biteback Publishing

*For Margaret Hilda Thatcher, without
whom none of this would have happened.*

First published in Great Britain in 2012 by
Biteback Publishing Ltd
Westminster Tower
3 Albert Embankment
London
SE1 7SP
Copyright © Madsen Pirie 2012

ISBN 978-1-84954-184-8

10 9 8 7 6 5 4 3 2 1

A CIP catalogue record for this book is available from the British Library.

Set in Garamond and Placard
Cover design by Namkwan Cho

Printed and bound in Great Britain by
TJ International, Padstow, Cornwall

CONTENTS

ACKNOWLEDGEMENTS

Several people helped with this book. Prominent among them is the team at Biteback Publishing, especially Iain Dale, Sam Carter and Hollie Teague. Essential help was freely given by my colleague, Eamonn Butler, whose story this also is, and who aided me in recording its incidents and detail. Daniel Cowdrill patiently read the early draft and made constructive comments on how it might be improved.

This is a very personal account, but the story it tells is one made by many people. It is my pleasure now to give thanks to all the young people who over the years have put time and effort into the work of the Adam Smith Institute. And finally I thank those who worked with the Institute from the political world, from academe, from business, from the media and from like-minded organizations, and whose contributions helped make these things happen.

Madsen Pirie
Cambridge 2012.

1

SHAPING AN INSTITUTE

It all began in the snows of Hillsdale, Michigan, where I was Professor of Philosophy. As the winter of 1976 drew to a close, there was change in the air in both Britain and America. Ronald Reagan was fighting for the Republican nomination he was finally to win three years later. Margaret Thatcher was Conservative leader in Britain. But there was more than this. The United States was gripped by its forthcoming bicentenary, as it prepared to celebrate the passage of 200 years since its first Independence Day.

In one of my syndicated US newspaper columns I pointed out that 1776 had been a significant year in several ways. It had marked the death of David Hume, the philosopher with whose ideas I had most sympathy. It saw the publication of volume I of *The Decline and Fall of the Roman Empire* by Edward Gibbon. In the same year James Watt had presented in Glasgow what was described as the first demonstration of a modern, efficient steam engine. On 4 July the American colonists had issued their Declaration of Independence. And by no means the least important event of the year: the book that virtually invented modern economics, *An Inquiry into the Nature and Causes of the Wealth of Nations* by the Scottish Enlightenment thinker Adam Smith, was published.

Smith had argued that countries were wealthy not because their rulers had gold and silver stored in vaults, but because of the productive labour of their peoples. He set out an account of how wealth can be created by the division of labour, and augmented by trade. He described the activities of investors, entrepreneurs and governments, and concluded that governments usually brought profligacy, rather than efficiency, into economic activity. His attack on subsidies, monopolies and all the trappings of government intervention seemed to have lessons for the modern world, and especially for Britain.

Stuart Butler (who was also teaching at Hillsdale), Eamonn Butler and I had all studied at the University of St Andrews, and had there helped to shape an ethos which had combined free-market economics with libertarian social attitudes. The usual combination on the political right was of a pro-business economic stance allied to paternalistic and restrictive social policies. We had no time for either, and had espoused pro-competition policies rather than ones friendly to established businesses, together with social policies that emphasized free choices and sanctioned alternative lifestyles.

All of us came from quite ordinary backgrounds and had attended state schools. We were all to some degree mischievous, even subversive, having no respect for established authority or position, but preferring to judge people on their abilities and ideas on their merit.

The University of St Andrews Conservative Association in which we were all involved had adopted these causes wholeheartedly, and turned itself into an effective force, spreading its ideas through meetings and publications both inside St Andrews and beyond. It acquired a national reputation for its espousal of this philosophy, and candidates imbued with those views began to run for local government and parliamentary elections.

We looked to Adam Smith as one of its intellectual forebears and, being part Scottish ourselves, drew added satisfaction from the fact that he, too, was Scottish. We had also been influenced by the works of such thinkers as Milton Friedman, Friedrich Hayek and Karl Popper.

There was an institute in London which drew heavily on Smith's ideas, and those of the free-market economists who had followed in his wake. This was the Institute of Economic Affairs (IEA), founded by Sir Antony Fisher twenty years earlier, and which had published a steady stream of monographs analyzing the deficiencies of central direction, state planning and economic intervention. They were intellectually rigorous, and had made their way into the literature of economics libraries, albeit in a separate corner, almost fenced off from the mainstream.

But we wanted something more. It was all very well to win theoretical arguments, but nothing seemed to happen afterwards. Governments continued on their unruly ways, while academics devised new follies to set up on the wreckage of the old ones. We wanted to change reality; to have an impact on what actually happened. We wanted to make policy.

Adam Smith might have been one strong influence on our thinking, but there were others. One was James Buchanan, the Nobel Laureate who, with Gordon Tullock, James Niskanen and others, developed what came to be known as Public Choice Theory. In essence it took the ideas of economics into the domain of politics and administration. Instead of treating politicians and civil servants as selfless seekers after public good, the theory treated them as if they were ordinary economic participants, out to maximize their own advantage, just like other people. It proved a very fertile theory for explaining what would otherwise have been incomprehensible outcomes. It also fitted in with the rather less than respectful way that we ourselves regarded politicians.

Public Choice told us how minority interest groups could hijack the political agenda to have advantages created for themselves. It explained how politicians respond to pressure from vociferous and self-interested groups, but not from a public at large which might be largely unconscious of the effect policy made upon it. Public Choice Theory was basically a critique, but we began to wonder if there could be a creative counterpart to it. Just as Public Choice Theory told us why certain policies were doomed to political failure, however economically sound they might be, could it not be used to create policies that would not be subject to these limitations? Could new free-market strategies be crafted that flowed with political reality by building in the support of the interest groups which might otherwise derail them?

This was powerful stuff. Sometime in the spring of 1976, Stuart Butler and I decided to return to the UK the following year to set up an institute to develop and propagate such policies. We had come to the US because it offered opportunities for employment and advancement scarcely possible in the UK of the 1970s. We had seen how vigorous was the drive for self-improvement in the US, and we had seen how US pressure groups and research organizations strove to create conditions under which it could flourish.

We wanted to replicate some of that in the UK, but the big problem was finance. There seemed to be no money for such a cause in Britain. There was no tradition of charitable giving in support of philosophical causes, nor any of the big foundations which supported research organizations in the US, nor any of the charity-friendly laws which had helped to promote philanthropy there.

With the naïveté of beginners, we blithely supposed that the US foundations would be only too eager to support such a worthy cause as the salvation of Britain. We sent proposals and arranged meetings with those who controlled the big bucks. We were helped hugely by Don Lipsett, who helped raise funds for Hillsdale College, and who also ran the Philadelphia Society, an organization which held annual conferences in the US to discuss free-market ideas. Don would regale us with stories of outrageous behaviour by those who ran charitable foundations, and liked few things better than planning strategy over dinners spent in good company.

He told us how to set out proposals, what to appeal to, and which words and phrases would resonate with particular organizations. More practically, he went through a list of likely prospects, briefing us on exactly whom to approach and how.

Thanks perhaps to his efforts, we were taken seriously by some foundations and not all of our letters were instantly put in the bin, though I suspect that most of them were. The few meetings we did have were unproductive. The foundation executives were unimpressed by our lack of a track record, the absence of other major supporters, and what they regarded as our completely unrealistic and over-optimistic budget proposals. They were right on all three and, not surprisingly, did not offer us any money. Plainly, if the institute were to get off the ground, it would have to do so without any backing from US donors.

We supposed we might eventually attract support in Britain, as the IEA did, but there were huge front-end costs to be met. We would need offices in London, office furniture and equipment and telephones. In addition we would need somewhere to live and some means of livelihood. It was a mountain to climb, and no one seemed inclined to help us up.

We began to consider alternative strategies. If we could not get help from the US to fund a policy institute in Britain, could we attract support for an academic institute to run parallel to it? The answer looked like no, because US charitable foundations were required to expend most of their funds in the US on domestic purposes. Furthermore, they had made it plain that if their interest did not extend beyond American shores, then neither would their cash.

Our next step attempted to overcome this parochialism on their part. If it could not be a British academic institute benefitting Britain, it could be an American one operating in Britain and catering for US students. The idea of spending a summer or a semester abroad, while earning credits towards a college degree, was beginning to spread in the 1970s, and there were several institutions which did this. We could hope to run such a programme, based on our experience at Hillsdale College.

We opted for a series of three-week summer courses held at Oxford and Cambridge. At three hours a day, these would each give the student three college credits. It would have been impossible to go through the accreditation process, and almost certainly unsuccessful, but we could piggy-back the courses onto Hillsdale's syllabus and use their accreditation. Our course enabled the college to add a summer abroad programme to its prospectus.

Students from other US colleges would come on our courses, gain Hillsdale credits and the college would receive part of the fee they paid. We hoped this academic programme would help finance the policy unit, which was our real goal. There were areas of overlap between the two, in that we expected both the academic programme and the policy research studies to feature the work of friendly UK scholars who shared our outlook.

We wasted some time investigating whether we could raise funds to take over what amounted to a ready-made university campus.

The Worldwide Church of God had put on sale its Ambassador College, in the north of London. It was just about the last word in luxury, with its purpose-built lecture theatres and enormous swimming pool. The blunt answer was that, no, we could not. There was no backing in either the UK or the US for such a grandiose, well-heeled venture. Sadly we had to settle for an organization which we could grow from nothing, rather than one we could take over fully equipped.

Our proposed institute began to take shape on more modest lines. Operating from London, it would advertise on US campuses for summer students. It would book space for three-week courses at Oxford and Cambridge, teaching the students fairly conventional subjects such as history, philosophy and literature. As a mainline academic institution catering for US students, it might hope to attract funds from US donors. Running parallel to it, from the same offices with the same personnel, would be a programme of innovative policy research designed to ally public choice ideas to those of free markets, perhaps providing solutions to some of Britain's long-term problems.

We had raised neither money nor the prospect of it, but were confident that we could. With the blessings of the Hillsdale College establishment we duly served out the year, attended the farewell parties and departed, with our belongings, on a Polish liner, the *Stefan Battory*, sailing for London out of Montreal. It was small, as liners go, and accepted all currencies except Polish zlotys. We were afterwards amused to read that on a later voyage the entire crew had jumped ship at Southampton rather than continue to live under communism.

The Hillsdale link was not entirely severed. Eamonn Butler had taken over my old job in Washington with the Republican Study Committee. Now the college was persuaded to hire him to take over my old job teaching philosophy. He even took on my house and my car, the antiquated gold-coloured Cadillac I had bought for a few hundred dollars. I used to tell audiences that it reminded me of home, being about the size of the house I was brought up in.

There was one last summer in Scotland, as we prepared to set up and operate our new institute in London. We needed a name and we needed premises. We decided initially on two names. The academic programme would be called the Adam Smith University, while the policy institute needed something a little less strident, and something which conjured up goodwill in the US as well as in Britain. We decided upon The Chatham Institute, since Pitt, Earl of Chatham, had been broadly sympathetic to the American colonists. We actually opened with that name in August of 1977, but found very rapidly that it was confused with the altogether more prestigious Chatham House. We also found, to our surprise, that very few Americans had any idea who the Earl of Chatham had been, whereas the name of Adam Smith attracted much more goodwill and support.

The Chatham Institute was quickly renamed the Adam Smith Institute, and ran more easily in parallel with the Adam Smith University. We registered the Institute as a US corporation in the state of Virginia, and both Stuart Butler and I kept our US green cards, allowing us to live and work in the United States whenever we wanted to. In truth, it is difficult to remember how bleak things seemed for Britain in the late 1970s. The economy was an international joke, and the trade unions swaggered about bullying everyone into meeting their demands.

One of our friends, telephoning family in South Africa, was surprised when a telephone engineer entered the conversation to say that because the call did not sound urgent, he was disconnecting it. The union had 'blacked' non-urgent calls to South Africa, and its members monitored private calls to enforce it.

More sinisterly, there were trade unionists and intellectuals who would rather have seen Britain as part of communist Eastern Europe rather than Western Europe, and there was genuine doubt at the time as to whether they might succeed. Both Stuart and I wished to keep our lifeline to the US. We said that if American helicopters came in to rescue their people ahead of the collapse, we wanted to be on them. We were joking, but only just.

It proved difficult to find premises. We had no money, just a few thousand dollars saved. We had received no backing at all. There were no donors or foundations to establish a bridgehead for these ideas in the UK, just us. With no income or assets, just limitless ambition, we did not qualify for mortgages. Furthermore, it was difficult from outside London to conduct a proper search. We went down to tramp the Westminster streets for ourselves.

We literally paced the streets, noting numbers from the estate agents' boards, and deciding where we wanted to be. It took us very little time to work out that we really needed to be within a ten-minute walk of the Houses of Parliament, located somewhere in the area of Westminster, Victoria or perhaps Pimlico. We stayed two nights with Rob Jones, an old St Andrews friend (who later became an MP and a Minister), out in Amersham and then, to cut travel times, we spent a day at a bed and breakfast house in Pimlico.

Everywhere was depressingly expensive, but at least we had an idea of what was available and how much we would have to try to raise. We were beginning to see nothing but problems when by chance, one of the estate agents indicated that there was a flat in Westminster already under offer to another bidder. We looked at it. A thirteen-year lease was available, the tail end of a longer one. It was in a residential block, but was in fact being used by four firms, each using a room kitted out as an office. There was a PR firm, a security company, one which sold financial services, and one which we never did work out what it did. The rooms had multiple telephone switchboards and neon lighting.

We considered our options rapidly. It was the summer of 1977. We had to start soon, and we had no money, no office, no salary, and nowhere to live in London. The Westminster place had advantages. It was within the requisite ten-minute walk of anywhere useful and within the division bell area of the House of Commons. While it did not look exactly smart, it might be made so. It had good transport links. It did not have a street entrance, however. Visitors had to climb a short flight of stairs to reach our door. There was no way we could put a brass plate outside and we would have to be discreet, given the residential status of the building. One huge advantage was that it was big enough to live in. It had a kitchen and a bathroom, both considerably faded from better days, shabby, indeed. But Stuart and I could each have a reasonably sized bedroom, leaving a huge living or reception room, and an office room. If we did not have to pay rent, we could live very cheaply, even in London. My years of poverty in St Andrews and Washington had taught me how to do that.

The place was under offer at £6,000 for the remainder of the thirteen-year lease. Quickly we decided to offer £6,500. It was all we had, but we still had our US credit cards and would be able perhaps to live on those until some cash came in. We offered instant cash, which I think proved at least as attractive in 1977 as did the extra £500. Our three days in London had proved remarkably successful. I returned to Scotland, Stuart to Shrewsbury, to await the outcome, and to get our Scottish lawyer friend on the case.

The deal was closed at high speed, with the settlement date fixed for the end of August. I paid one more visit to London to check out the place and take measurements. I saw, to my surprise, that the previous occupants were taking away everything that could be pried loose, including towel rails. They left the carpets and curtains only because they were so old and musty that it might have been a health hazard to remove them. They were of a colour that had started life as a kind of dark beige and grown steadily darker over the decades. I thought optimistically that we could slowly redecorate the place over time, perhaps doing a lot of the work ourselves. On the good side, the place did have central heating, which was by no means common in the UK at the time.

That final August in St Andrews was a good one. I was staying in a house with its own rose garden and had the good company of one of my old Hillsdale students, Steve Masty, a man of letters who seemed to have slipped out of the 1930s by mistake who, inspired by the scholar Russell Kirk and me, was undertaking a postgraduate degree there. The weather was perfect, and there were forays to be made into the Fife countryside and coastline. The clock was ticking, but pleasantly.

On 30 August I travelled down to stay with Rob Jones for one more night, carrying as much as I could in two suitcases and sending a trunk ahead. I met up with Stuart and we took possession of the Westminster property the following afternoon. That night, the last day of August 1977, we slept on camp beds in a place totally bare, apart from its strip lights. There was no furniture, crockery or cutlery. But the Adam Smith Institute was open for business.

2

MAKING CONTACTS

The first few weeks of the Adam Smith Institute presented a hectic mix of intellectual and administrative activity combined with simple housekeeping. There were challenges to be overcome every day on all of these fronts. We needed furniture. It was fine in theory to live in the office because it meant that we could work without salary. Without rent to pay, and having learned to live cheaply, the Institute's personnel did not have to add their living expenses to its overheads.

In practice this meant solving elementary problems such as having somewhere to sit and something to eat from. Tea chests and camp beds were fine for a short time, but the place had to be made both habitable and presentable. Stuart Butler and I both had our electric typewriters from Hillsdale, complete with transformers to let them work on UK voltage, but we needed desks to put them on and chairs to sit at.

Our supplies came from three sources. Through the magazine *Exchange and Mart* we learned of an office supply shop just across the river in Lambeth. Its cheap and second-hand goods were piled on the pavement outside. We equipped ourselves with two basic tables and chairs for almost nothing. There was a second-hand bunk bed which, taken apart, made two perfectly serviceable, if narrow, beds for us to sleep on. They lasted many years, and were even taken to Cambridge to serve Eamonn's growing children many years later.

There was always building going on in London, as there still is. Builders' skips outside of properties being demolished or renovated provided a ready source of free wood for bookcases and shelves. The dependable *Exchange and Mart* identified cheap metal angle shelving that lasted us many years. These sources supplied most of our office needs.

The main source of our needed domestic supplies was unexpected. My two aunts, learning about our venture, volunteered surplus furniture. One was in Hull, one Cleethorpes, so Stuart and I hired a small van and headed off first to South Yorkshire, then to North Lincolnshire. It was a rich haul: we collected a sofa and two armchairs, various small tables and chairs, a rocking chair, plus a bureau and supplies of crockery, cutlery and kitchen tools.

Calling at Hull first, we then crossed the Humber on the ferry boat, *Tattershall Castle*, as I had done several times during my childhood. It is now moored on London's Embankment as a floating pub. By the time we left Cleethorpes the van was totally packed, but it did kit out the ASI and make it a habitable, if slightly shabby and outdated, living space.

We needed a telephone and a photo-copier. We were told by the Post Office, which ran the state monopoly telephone service, that there was a fourteen-month wait to have a line and phone installed. We somehow bargained them into doing it within six weeks by pointing out that our predecessors in the building had used a switchboard with four separate telephone numbers, one for each of the companies that had used the place, and all we wanted to do was to re-activate one line. Until the GPO engineers came, we had to conduct all the new Institute's business from the public call box on the corner, and we ensured we kept a ready supply of coins for the purpose.

The Post Office would not let us buy a phone; we had to rent one from them. This was their standard practice. The instrument they graciously allowed us to rent was a black, Bakelite instrument with a rotary dial, designed in the 1930s. For this magnificent piece of equipment we had to pay a quarterly rental of £14.65, or just under £60 a year. We overcame the problem by rewiring the place ourselves with extensions, and buying US phones on our visits there, complete with conversion sockets. This was contrary to all the Post Office rules, but it worked. And it meant that we were among the first in Britain to use such gadgets as recall dialling, wireless remotes and one-button dialling of our most-used numbers.

We needed a photo-copier but couldn't afford one. The cheapest rental was a rotary Xerox machine which involved placing your original sheet into a plastic folder which was fed into the machine, and then came out with a copy. This was not only very slow, but would not work for anything that could not fit into the folder. You could not copy a page from a book or a newspaper, for example. Our biggest scare was of power cuts, which still tended to happen occasionally during bouts of strike action. If the power died mid-copying, the original would be stuck inside the machine until power was restored.

ADAM SMITH UNIVERSITY PROGRAMME

It seems surprising that with such limited equipment we were able to organize anything at all, but we managed somehow. Our first task was to set up the Adam Smith University programme and recruit US students for summer study in Britain. Their up-front payments would give us the cash flow to tide us over until we could attract support or generate revenue.

We visited Oxford and Cambridge to inspect colleges and sign up for our students to stay three weeks at each during the following summer. It was quite an eye-opening experience to see the leisurely pace of life in both places, and included pleasant afternoons punting on the river when the day's business was done. We signed up for three weeks at St Edmund's Hall, Oxford, and the same at Magdalene College, Cambridge.

We had to recruit US students, with the allure of spending three glorious summer weeks in the UK, while picking up three credits towards their own degree. We used our contacts from the Mont Pelerin Society and the Institute of Economic Affairs, plus free-market academics whose works we had read, and even one of my old lecturers from Edinburgh, to teach our courses. It was very much a cobbled-together team but they were all talented academics and some were quite prestigious; and it enabled us to establish contact with like-minded academics from UK universities.

Having visited Oxford and Cambridge universities, we decided they were more of a draw than our own as-yet-unknown Adam Smith University programme, so our brochure featured idyllic photographs of the colleges. We mailed them in bulk from within the US to as many colleges and universities as we could afford, asking the dean to put them up on college notice-boards. At one point I visited the States and toured South Carolina, visiting its colleges, interviewing their deans, leaving leaflets and promoting our programme.

Gradually students wrote in to register for our courses at Oxford or Cambridge, but not as many as we had hoped. We did, however, attract just enough to make the effort viable, and their advance cheques kept the ASI afloat until we worked out how we would pay the bills afterwards.

The summer schools themselves were great fun. We decamped first to Magdalene College, Cambridge, for three weeks, and then for another three to St Edmund's Hall in Oxford. While the teaching itself from the academics we had hired was excellent, the general ambience of those weeks was also very enjoyable for us. We employed two UK student helpers and ate meals in college with the US students, reliving our own student days.

During each three-week course we organized a weekend trip to Boulogne, to give most of our students their first taste of continental Europe and of a foreign-speaking country. We went over on the hovercraft and stayed in cheap bed and breakfast accommodation. We took them sightseeing and dining, and brought back cheeses and wines for an impromptu party on the train home after we'd crossed the Channel.

We were able to do this, effectively shutting down the ASI for a few weeks while we did so, because we were still building up the Institute. The contacts we made with the academics were immensely important for our future plans. In any case, I doubt if anyone even noticed we were gone from London. When Parliament closes down for nearly three months in the summer, there is a general slowing-down of public policy activity. We could disappear into the academic world without anyone finding out.

ST JAMES SOCIETY

We wanted to hold conferences. In the US the Philadelphia Society's annual conferences acted as a get-together for like-minded people of the free-market persuasion. We needed something similar in the UK and decided to launch a similar organization with a big weekend seminar. It was a good way of networking with others on our side.

We joined forces with the IEA and the Centre for Policy Studies (CPS) and organized conferences at the St James Court hotel in Westminster, which was then somewhat down at heel, but quite cheap to stay in. Somewhat unimaginatively we called our group the St James Society. As speakers we signed up free-market political figures such as Sir Geoffrey Howe and Sir Keith Joseph, plus columnists and academics who shared our outlook. The highlight of the first conference was a debate between Brian Walden, an ex-Labour MP and ITV's *Weekend World* presenter, and John O'Sullivan, a sketch writer for the *Daily Telegraph*. Surprisingly, Walden took a conservative position against O'Sullivan's radical Hayekism.

One gripping moment came when Sir Keith Joseph first introduced the idea of enterprise zones, a policy the then Conservative opposition was preparing in the event of it winning the next election.

At the final dinner of the second St James conference, when we presented Sir Geoffrey Howe with a framed Roman penny bearing the head of the emperor Claudius II, we told Sir Geoffrey that the coin was clipped at the edges, underlining the importance of preserving the value of honest money. It featured a great victory arch on one side, a portent perhaps for the coming election. We also pointed out that it was said of the emperor whose likeness it bore that 'after two years of weak and vacillating government he was assassinated by his own troops'. Sir Geoffrey said he would remember those messages 'selectively'.

There were at that time very few people who thought that free-market ideas and economic incentives could succeed in turning Britain around, and the St James Society brought them together from the think tanks, the universities and Parliament itself. Most were in a tiny minority in their own institutions, and meetings like those of the St James Society enabled them to feel the comfort of numbers. We used to point out that you could then fit most of us into a taxi, and that the entire free-market movement would be wiped out if it crashed.

We organized a further two St James conferences, keeping the name though changing the location. One we held in the Manor House Hotel in Oxford and one in the National Liberal Club in London. As with the opening one, they were fully booked because of the degree of co-operation we were able to achieve on the centre-right. We slipped easily into working with the IEA, the CPS and the National Federation of Small Businesses. We all got on well and occasionally ate out together. We were all conscious of how few of us there were.

It was a huge help that we had some press support. The *Telegraph* sketch writers, John O'Sullivan and Frank Johnson were very much on side, as were leader writers from the *Telegraph*, *The Times*, the *Daily Mail* and others. We had hardly any friends in radio or television, however.

A group of us took to meeting at Saturday lunchtime in the Cork and Bottle wine bar just off Leicester Square, owned by New Zealander Don Hewitson. We would colonize one of the barrel-vaulted alcoves and eat lunch together as we planned strategy for the week ahead. Those meetings always included the ASI and someone from the IEA and the CPS, plus people from *The Times* and *Telegraph*, from Margaret Thatcher's research staff (and later the No. 10 Policy Unit), and occasionally visiting friends from the US. We would eat Provence Salad or Jean's 'famous raised ham and cheese pie', and drink Australian wines, not then as fashionable as they subsequently became, usually rounding off with a glass of Brown Bothers liqueur Muscat.

Typically we would decide how we could focus the policy agenda onto specific subjects during the coming weeks and try to co-ordinate our activities to make us more effective collectively than we would have been individually. One or more of the think tanks might arrange a publication; another would organize a seminar; the journalists would endeavour to have the subject covered in leader columns; while the research staff would ensure it was drawn to the attention of the appropriate members of the shadow Cabinet.

IUOS

Another activity we organized jointly with the other think tanks was designed to provide a focus for students who shared free-market or libertarian values, and who found themselves heavily outnumbered in the fashionable left-wing activism of the day. As with the St James Society, the idea was for a national forum that would make students aware that they were part of a larger group.

The idea was not to reflect Conservatism, which had been rather sullied by the legacy of Edward Heath, and was not yet redeemed by the experience of Margaret Thatcher. Instead we chose to reflect the ideas of liberal thinkers such as Friedrich Hayek and Karl Popper. The latter's classic work, *The Open Society and its Enemies*, inspired the title of our effort. We called it the *International University of the Open Society*, and decided that it would take the form of a residential week at a Cambridge College, with an intensive programme of lectures and workshops.

Our experience of the Adam Smith University summer programme for US students proved quite useful for the organization of the IUOS, as it came to be known, and we recruited Sam Stewart, a friend who had been bursar at Swinton Conservative College, to act as its organizer. Sam was an ex-Second World War submariner who had spent most of the war as a prisoner, and who had been present at one of the famous escape plots dramatized in the movie, *Albert, RN* (the name given to the dummy that fooled the Germans). He would entertain the students with stories of his experiences.

This annual Cambridge week gave us a relaxed but rewarding few days making contact with the next generation of liberal-minded students. We spiced up its social appeal by including punting afternoons and treasure hunts in its otherwise serious programme. Several people like John Whittingdale, who later entered Parliament, first met us at these Cambridge seminars. The effort of organization and raising the few thousand pounds they cost was justified by the results, because it built up a network of committed young people that we were able to draw on for years afterwards.

One input the students contributed was their view that the word 'University' was somewhat pretentious for what was in reality a one-week conference. We agreed, and changed it to the *International Symposium on the Open Society*, or ISOS, an acronym that had the advantage of being easier to pronounce.

TAKING STOCK

As we came towards the end of the first year of the Adam Smith Institute, we took stock of our progress. We had not made much of an impact. We had held no large-scale conferences to generate news stories that might publicize our ideas. We had produced no publications and had made no media appearances on radio or television. On the other hand we had established our presence within the policy and think tank worlds. By the St James Society conferences and the student seminars we had made the Adam Smith Institute known to insiders, if not yet to the public at large.

Moreover, our contacts with university lecturers and professors in connection with our Adam Smith University summer programmes had given us access to speakers and writers for our future activities. And our contacts with sympathetic journalists had given us the prospect of media coverage when we did eventually produce something worth covering.

Unfortunately we had also run out of money. The bank's letters were becoming more strident and it was an increasing struggle to meet the bills for the premises. The short-term solution to this was for me to return to Hillsdale. Since Eamonn was coming back to the UK, I could take my old job back for a single semester, earning enough money to keep the ASI going for perhaps another year. In late August of 1978, I returned for a final teaching spell at Hillsdale, returning to London in mid-December.

This gave me the chance to teach philosophy and logic to a new generation of students, and to enjoy for a few months more the academic lifestyle. Autumn is much the best part of the year in southern Michigan, and I had a happy time making new friends among the students.

It marked a major shift for the ASI, since Stuart decided to return to the US to live and work there. He secured an important post at the Heritage Foundation as Director (and later Vice President) of Domestic Policy. Stuart found the financial uncertainty in Britain depressing and thought he would be more comfortable in a well-paid job in the US.

It meant that his brother Eamonn replaced him at the Adam Smith Institute. When I returned to the UK in late 1978, I had enough money to keep the Institute going, but it was Eamonn, rather than Stuart, who would be my colleague in the coming decades.

Although the additional money brought some relief, it by no means solved our problems. The cash being paid up front for the summer schools we held for US students helped with our cash flow, but it was only cash flow, since we had to pay the bills to the colleges we stayed at. We were still not attracting enough funds to make the ASI a viable organization, and everything we did had to be done with one eye on the bottom line measuring what we could afford. We even installed a device mounted under our phone that showed us how much calls, particularly international calls, were costing us. In the days before telephone privatization, that could be a large amount.

On some occasions we managed to stave off legal action at the last minute by drawing cash from a new credit card, and we often drew money on one credit card to pay the bill on another one. Living on a credit card was a very good way of kicking the can forward. We could worry about paying the bills later, but of course they grew larger.

We benefited by chance from our days at St Andrews. While there we had bought a derelict cottage for £60. It had been a weaver's cottage originally and was far too small ever to be made habitable. We had used it as a kind of club house and storage room for the University Conservative Association. After I left, but while Eamonn was still there, I used to spend summers in St Andrews, and during one of them we tracked down the US owner of the adjacent cottage, who was completely surprised to find that he owned a derelict cottage in St Andrews. At the back of our minds was the thought that with two cottages we might knock them together to make a viable dwelling.

We successfully bid £1,100 for the adjacent property out of money I'd earned at Hillsdale, and held on to the two of them for a few years. As we were living and working in London and trying to build up the ASI, we received an enquiry from St Andrews and eventually an offer to buy the two cottages by a would-be developer. We decided to sell, and to use the proceeds to help fund the Institute. The sale yielded nearly £10,000, which in the late 1970s was a small fortune, practically twice the average annual wage, and it was tax free.

WINDSOR CONFERENCES

Unexpected help with our finances came our way when we were able to organize joint conferences with a US foundation. We had met its leaders at Mont Pelerin and Philadelphia Society conferences. This was a group active in the US (and quite well funded), which campaigned for the right of US workers not to join or be represented by labour unions and for employers who did not wish to be compelled to employ union labour.

The organization was somewhat controversial, even in the US, since it was widely opposed, even detested, by many Democrats who depended heavily on labour union money and election workers to run their elections. In Britain at the time, in the grip of union power, it was regarded as beyond the pale. However, we were already actively working to limit union power in Britain, and saw joint conferences with the US group as a symbiotic relationship.

They wanted to run a conference in Britain for their top people and asked us to organize it for them. They wanted a prestigious location, so we suggested St George's House within Windsor Castle, which we knew was anxious to expand its facilities as a conference venue in order to bring in extra revenue. This was not quite as easy at it seemed, because the accommodation at St George's House was decidedly less than luxurious by US standards. There were no showers, for example, so we had to buy the plastic ones which could be connected to the antiquated St George's House bath taps. There were no hair dryers, so we bought in a dozen from Boots. Some guests had to double up, which was not something pampered American donors were used to. Our hope was that the conferees from the US would settle for less than luxury for the trade-off of staying in a royal palace.

For the programme itself we brought in some of the academics we had established links with through our other programmes. They included Professor Kenneth Minogue, an expert in ideology from the London School of Economics, Dr Arthur Shenfield and a very bright young specialist in industrial relations, Dr John Burton. Building up links with US specialists as well, the programme was put together with speakers the US group brought over.

Our theme was by no mean limited to employment law. On the contrary, we set out much of the centre-right agenda, ranging from privatization to the discounted sale of state council houses.

To add some balance to the programme we invited Arthur Scargill, widely tipped as the favourite to succeed Joe Gomley as head of the National Union of Mineworkers. He put the case for the union side. He was widely regarded as a visceral Marxist. Yet it was revealing that when he talked of his own struggles in coal-mining and his rise from an impoverished background, he was eloquent and enthralling, but when he gave a Marxist overview of the current UK scene it was like turning on a recording of strung-together left-wing clichés. I also noted that the three jokes he told all hinged on his being mistaken for God.

Privately, and over dinner in Windsor town, he was relaxed and quite charming, and showed considerable taste in wines and fine foods. When I asked him if he'd thought of running for Parliament, he dismissed the idea with scorn, saying he was going to stay where the real power was – in the Trade Union movement. It was during one of those conferences that we received news that NUM leader Joe Gormley had announced his intention to resign. Scargill confirmed to us, eyes shining, that he was going to run.

The conferees loved the mixture of old Britain in a royal palace and the new Britain we were determined to make with free-market reforms. They were indeed prepared to put up with a lack of luxury in order to be in Windsor Castle. The ASI, including the two students we'd hired to help out, stayed nearby at the Star and Garter Hotel in order to free up more castle rooms for our US visitors.

We hammed up old Britain for their benefit. The St George's Library in which we held our sessions had Tudor gothic windows high above the castle walls, great wooden beams and high ceilings, and was lined with bookcases that included a 1481 edition of Caxton. In my introduction I explained that the room had seen the premiere of Shakespeare's *Merry Wives of Windsor* in the presence of Elizabeth I. I would point to a chair one of the American ladies was occupying on the front row and say dramatically, 'Queen Elizabeth sat *there*.' The Americans would draw in their breath at the thought of such proximity to royalty, even with a time gap of 400 years. It was true about the premiere, though not about the chair.

I also cautioned them that if they returned to the castle at night after visiting the town, and were challenged by a sentry armed with a semi-automatic rifle, it did not really matter what they said, as long as they said it quickly. We were given a conducted tour of the publicly accessible parts of the castle and invited to attend Evensong sitting in the choir stalls in St George's Chapel. It was at a service there that I suddenly sat bolt upright when the Dean of the Chapter of St George's said, 'May the Lord bless the work of the Adam Smith Institute.' Apparently this is a courtesy normally extended to groups holding conferences there, but I mischievously suggested to Eamonn that we should add it to our list of quotes that people had made about the Institute.

So naïve were we that it only gradually dawned on us why the

US group was holding these conferences. They were bringing some of their biggest donors over to the UK to reward them for their support, and to attract more contributions from them and their friends. It raised our awareness of how important fund-raising is in maintaining the work of institutes, and how much time and effort the American think tanks invested in it. We learned a great deal by observing their methods.

We finally realized what was going on when they had a session devoted to 'maintaining the effort', which puzzled us until we worked out that it was all about making wills and leaving the organization a legacy to continue its causes after their (mostly elderly) donors had passed on. We derived much merriment from the fact that their director in charge of this effort came on to make his speech wearing a black suit and tie, looking for all the world like a funeral director. Moreover, he spoke in sonorous, one might say funereal, tones about what people might leave behind. We decided this might be somewhat over the top for us to try with a British audience.

There was a quite unpleasant end to the association, and one that caused us much distress and difficulty. We had been urged to spend money on things like chauffeured limousines from London, only to have complaints that we were over budget. After the conference ended we began receiving a few cheques from some of the conferees we had befriended and apparently impressed. They were all wealthy Americans who were accustomed to supporting causes they believed in.

The cheques were mostly for $1,000 each, and made out to the Adam Smith Institute. Our US conference co-hosts heard about this and insisted we hand over all such monies to them. There had been no agreement to do this because neither of us had anticipated this would happen. However, since they had organized and funded the conference it seemed reasonable to us that any given in support for the conference, or in appreciation of it, should be sent on to them. We could not reassign the cheques, but we could pay them an equivalent amount.

We were somewhat disturbed our American colleagues insisted that we hand over all payment received by us from those who had attended the conference, even when they made it clear that it was us they wanted to assist. What caused us most difficulty was that each time we attempted to reach a fair settlement it was treated by them as the basis for further demands. Even when donors wrote praising our work and expressing a wish to support us as well as them, we were expected to hand over the money without telling the donors we had done so. This seemed deceitful as well as unjust.

The problem for us was that we had assumed we would be keeping some of these donations when we planned our budget. Having to hand them over left us short of funds to pay our bills with, including those from the summer school colleges. It taught us an important lesson, and while we subsequently held joint conferences with other organizations, including US ones, we never did so again with that particular group, and never did so again based on a mere understanding or a gentleman's agreement. Everything in future had to be spelled out.

The summer schools, the Open Society symposium, the St James Society and joint conferences at Windsor all helped to establish our presence within the narrow world of think tanks and liberal-minded academics, but we had yet to make our mark on the national scene. That would take publications, policy research that mattered and media coverage. We had achieved none of these so far, but all that was about to change.

3

MAKING A MARK

The winter of 1978–9 was the so-called 'Winter of Discontent', when many public sector workers, including many in local government, took strike action. In many cities rubbish bags piled up in huge mounds: Leicester Square in London was covered in hundreds of black bags. In some cities the dead were left unburied as municipal graveyard and crematorium workers went on strike. One widely reported case saw ambulance personnel leave their patients in the snow when a radio message instructed them to go on strike.

It was against this backdrop that the first publication of the Adam Smith Institute drew closer to being ready for release. It was a book entitled *The Trojan Horse* by John Burton, a rising young labour relations economist, and was a study of the impact of trade union power in British politics. John was totally unpretentious, a snappy dresser with a Northern accent and a taste for Lea and Perrins sauce over most of his food. His writing was just as spiced with wit and insights.

John identified what he called the 'power vortex', in which, over beer and sandwiches at 10 Downing Street, Labour governments would agree to increase the powers of labour unions, which in turn would use those powers to help elect Labour governments.

For example, unions had been granted the right to impose an automatic political levy on their members. While members could opt out in theory, they were exposed to pressure and even intimidation if they did so. The funds thus accumulated were used to back Labour Party candidates and to help fund the Labour Party at a national level. And Labour governments stood ready to enact yet more legislation favourable to trade unions; so powerful were the unions that they felt they had no choice.

John's research delved into the origin and history of trade union powers, showing how their long symbiotic relationship with Labour governments had equipped them with huge powers to extort cash and benefits from employers and taxpayers and to act against the public good. It had left the British people with no redress against them or any means of restraining their power. The book was powerful stuff, and could not have been better timed if we had planned it that way.

In fact we had commissioned it from John long before the Winter of Discontent had made it so topical. It was a happy coincidence for us that it came out in mid-January, 1979, amid a sea of outrageous strikes and union demands. There was a general feeling in Britain that something would have to be done.

We designed a cover showing a photograph of a union march with a black panel above it bearing its title in reversed out lettering, with a white strip separating the two. Without knowing it we had developed what was to become our distinctive house style for years to come. At a time when most policy pamphlets came in plain covers with traditional black lettering, ours looked more akin to the popular novels that filled the stands in bookshops and newsagents. It was more populist – even sexy, as some of our critics put it.

We had a rough idea of what it might take to attract press interest. We worked out that what journalists wanted was probably a press release of no more than a page and a half which summarized the main points of the publication, picked out a few pithy quotes and had a snappy heading that would attract their interest. We also calculated that they might want to receive it, with a copy of the book, a few days in advance of the embargoed release date, but not much more than that or they would simply set it aside as not being immediately relevant.

We made no attempt to send it to the editors of book pages or to attract book reviews for it, but concentrated entirely on it as a news event rather than a book. Thus it went to news editors, political editors, labour relations correspondents and economics writers. We used a scatter-gun technique, sending out several copies to all the main daily newspapers, plus the Press Association and other press agencies. We guessed that if a wire story appeared about it, it would encourage journalists at least to take a look at our press release, if not the actual book.

We had no secretarial help and no franking machine, so this exercise involved us in much filling of envelopes, licking of stamps and trips to the Post Office carrying armfuls of packets. It was quite a costly operation, too, for an organization that had no money, as well as being very time-consuming.

However, it paid off. The *Daily Telegraph* phoned us to ask if John Burton would write them a feature article to publish on the day of its release. He readily agreed, and in fact had two feature articles on their editorial page on successive days. Crucially, at the foot of these articles came what we started to call the magic three words: Adam Smith Institute. We needed to establish our presence. Moreover the *Telegraph* wrote leaders on the subject, mentioning the book and the Institute itself. There was other coverage in other papers, but none as spectacular as that in the *Telegraph*. And because it was the paper of choice of much of the Conservative Party, sometimes jocularly dubbed the *Torygraph*, it meant that we were able to get our message across to the party.

Eamonn and I had many tactical discussions about how the ASI should operate. We decided to do so in the public domain, not advising MPs and shadow ministers in private, but talking to them publicly via the media. This meant we would need a very high media profile and would have to work to gain coverage for our ideas. We needed to have our ideas and proposals talked about by columnists and commentators.

The advantage of doing it this way was that the ideas could be discussed in public and become familiar and understood. That in turn made it easier for them to be taken up by politicians as policy initiatives, and it also meant the proposals could be improved by the commentators who discussed them, so by the time any were adopted there had already been discussion of how they might be applied.

We used to say that 'the best idea in the world will be ineffective if only the milkman ever gets to hear of it'. This was not to denigrate milkmen, but to indicate that we needed our target audience to become aware of our ideas and to give them consideration if we were to achieve any impact. In other words we would have to shout.

Again unwittingly we were creating our own house style. Instead of trying to capture the ears and attention of legislators and civil servants privately, we were talking to them publicly through the pages of the media. Our ideal model was to have news stories feature our published policy ideas, and then have legislators and civil servants ask for copies to be sent to them. That happened less often than we would have liked, but we did manage to put most of our publications and proposals into the public domain.

Private companies would order single copies; bookshops three; government departments would send round a book agent on foot to collect five or six; quangos sent round motorcycle couriers to pick up a dozen.

Although we were putting our ideas out to the public at large through media coverage, it was not them we were aiming at. While it was certainly useful if we could help to shape public opinion, we were very conscious that this was not our primary task. It was a bonus. We identified our real audience as those who might loosely be called opinion formers and opinion leaders. This included MPs, and especially frontbenchers and prominent backbenchers. Added to them were their special advisers and senior research assistants. Then we included some civil servants, especially those in departments we wanted to influence. In addition to all these were the media personnel, the editors, the political and economics correspondents and the regular columnists we might interest in our ideas. There were a few people in the broadcast media as well, but our observation was that the radio and television agenda was very much set by what had appeared in the newspapers.

At one stage we did a head count and calculated that the number of people whose attention we sought amounted to about 650 people. We thought that 666 would have been a more resonant and significant number, but the point was that we were broadcasting our material to millions in order to reach a few hundred. Many people not on that list sought copies of our publications, which we duly supplied, but we charged them to cover the costs of printing and postage. We wanted to get copies into as many hands as possible. The result was that selling books became a large part of our activity, and the cheques that arrived daily in payment mounted up to make a worthwhile contribution to our funds.

The political establishment did not quite know what to make

of the Adam Smith Institute. It had appeared out of nowhere and started to make noises. It had no pedigree and no background in UK universities or journalism. Somehow a group of outsiders had set up in Westminster and was striving to influence national policy. While some in the Conservative Party regarded us as benign, others were less than pleased at what we were doing. It was not long before commentators like Norman St John Stevas were talking about the 'poison cloud' hovering about the party. We rather liked the description.

THE ASI BOARDS

Since we were now establishing our presence in the eyes of the political and media worlds, we felt we needed respectability. All other institutes seemed to have academic advisory boards, so we decided to assemble one of our own. Since we were upstarts, we had no idea if respectable people would agree to have their names linked with ours.

To our great delight the Nobel economics laureate, Professor F. A. Hayek, whom we knew and revered through the Mont Pelerin Society, agreed to be the chairman of our board of scholars. With him in place it became easy to secure the assent of others to place their names beside him on our headed paper. The academic board never actually met as a group, though most of its members knew each other. Among the prestigious names we recruited were Professor Kenneth Minogue and Professor William Letwin, both of LSE's Department of Government, and Dr Arthur Shenfield, a much respected and widely published scholar in the classical liberal tradition.

Their consent to having their names associated with us gave us a gravitas which we otherwise lacked. We decided from the beginning to continue using our own academic titles to emphasize our scholarly background. At a time when free-market ideas were thought to be simply impractical and lacking in serious import, Eamonn and I both thought it would be an advantage to use the 'Doctor' prefix to our names to which our PhDs entitled us and, while my association with Hillsdale continued, I sometimes used the 'Professor' title they awarded me. Antony Fisher, the serial entrepreneur who had founded the Institute of Economic Affairs, described PhDs as being 'like holy water'.

Our corporate structure was much less easy to settle. Any potential donors, be they individuals or institutions, would want to see our annual report and take a look at who was associated with us. We needed a few heavyweights they would respect and a structure that fitted in with what they were used to. Other think tanks in the UK and the US seemed mostly to have charitable status. In the US this was called 501(C)(3) status after the appropriate tax clauses, and meant that contributions to such bodies could be taken off gross income when it was declared for tax purposes.

It was more complex in the UK, allowing the tax that had been paid on contributions to be reclaimed at the basic rate. The IEA was a 'charity' qualifying for that label under the heading of 'public education'. Putting out policy research and proposals qualified as educating the public and within the ambit of 'charitable purposes'.

We did not like this very much because the average person in the street thought of charity in terms of widows and orphans and aiding the sick and disadvantaged. To use the label for public policy research might seem to the public at large like an abuse of the term and as if we were using the tax system to promote political causes.

We settled on three distinct identities. One was our US-registered body for which we sought and obtained the coveted 501(C)(3) status. One was ASI Research Ltd, a company trading as the Adam Smith Institute, and one was the Adam Smith Research

Trust, registered as a charitable trust and devoted to educational purposes. It was a very messy patchwork and it took us years to sort it out. We used the term 'Adam Smith Institute' loosely to cover all our activities, no matter which heading they occurred under. The important thing was that our publications were issued under the imprint of ASI Research Ltd, because if we inadvertently published a libel, the company could only be sued for its share capital of £100.

Neither Eamonn nor I had any clear idea about company and charity law, and we found it complex and opaque. We were total amateurs just wanting to do the right thing, but we knew our activities would be controversial and we wanted to protect both the Institute and ourselves from any hostile action. Our interest was *policy* rather than *politics*.

In both the US and the UK we had seen how internal power struggles could destroy an organization and divert it from its primary purpose. We were determined that this should never happen to the Adam Smith Institute, and settled for a governing structure that would be impervious to such activity.

The nominal share capital of the ASI was distributed between friends and family. Ownership and control boiled down to me and Eamonn, and no one else. We were also the trustees of the charity and the directors of both the US and the UK bodies. Our governing board was an advisory board whose brief was to assist and advise the two directors, who were not compelled to take its advice.

It was an awkward and clunky system, but it worked reasonably well in practice and gave us the freedom to take the Institute pretty well where we wanted to. Neither of us at that stage drew a salary or even any significant expenses from the ASI; there simply was not the money.

Throughout the entire history of the ASI we were never subjected to a power struggle or an attempted takeover. The appropriate levers of power were just not there to be grasped. Our board was happy with their advisory role, and never once did they attempt to force on the directors a decision we opposed, and never once did we ignore advice they had given. Perhaps it was because we had carefully chosen people with whom we could get along, and whose opinion we respected. In fact it was a good match. We valued greatly the help the board gave and they liked the impact the Institute managed to achieve.

Both Eamonn and I had worked briefly (though at different times) in Washington for the Republican Study Committee on Capitol Hill, which was an association of members of Congress on the conservative side of the spectrum. They pooled some of their staff allowance to create a small research team headed by Edwin J. Feulner Jr. He had gone on to become President of the Heritage Foundation and had subsequently turned it into an immensely powerful and influential organization. Now he agreed to serve briefly as an adviser while we built up the board's strength. It was a big plus.

We sought people with experience of UK business and whose names commanded respect within the business community. One such was Edgar Palamountain, head of the M&G securities group and the Esmee Fairbairn Charitable Trust, who supported a variety of free-market causes and was happy to add the Adam Smith Institute to that list.

Another was Antony Fisher, who had founded the Institute of Economic Affairs, following advice from F. A. Hayek. Hayek had told him that a research organization founded to propagate free-market ideas would be more worthwhile than a foray into politics. He was not initially on our board, but readily agreed to join us a little later, and was sufficiently well connected to attract other people with business reputations to participate. It was he who suggested the name of Bob Bee as our first chairman. It was a brilliant one because Bob, an American banker living and working in London, was a real live-wire who combined commitment with energy and expertise. He had run a successful private bank and wanted to help the cause of freedom and a free economy. He in turn suggested a couple of others who might want to help.

Now we had some names supporting our cause we looked respectable enough, but we knew that most people glossed over the names of worthies associated with organizations. It was all very well putting illustrious names on our letterheads, leaflets and on the flyleaf of our publications, but it did not count for very much. If it failed to impress us when we saw it done by others, we guessed it probably would not impress them either when we did it. We knew that it would be our output that mattered.

It was time to let the business community know about us. Eamonn acquired a second-hand repeating typewriter from a shop in Oxford. It was driven by a paper tape and was very cumbersome, but Eamonn worked out how to use sticky tape to make a loop out of the paper tape so it could type the same letter to all the top companies. We topped and tailed it to each of 200 of them, describing the Adam Smith Institute and asking them to help financially. People were not at that stage used to automated letters, so they presumed each one had been hand typed. About twenty of them replied, sending us cheques. They were not large sums, but some of those early subscribers stayed with us for decades.

AUSTRIAN ECONOMICS

We took a decision early on to try to keep one foot in the world of academe. It helped that we ran the summer schools at Oxford and Cambridge for American students, but we decided to produce, in addition to our researched policy proposals, more academic and philosophical works relating to Austrian School economics and the merits of markets and trade. This was the economic school developed by Ludwig von Mises, Friedrich Hayek and others, which saw economics as a process that conveyed information participants could act on. It was very free market and skeptical of most government intervention, especially that which tried to steer the economy. It never bothered us that although we bore the name of Scotland's founder of modern economics, we ourselves subscribed to the Austrian School. Some saw irony in that and commented to us on it.

Our second publication, coming a month or so after *The Trojan Horse*, was *The Suffolk Bank*, an academic history of the Suffolk Bank. This had been a private bank operating in Virginia, which had taken unto itself the role of a central clearing bank in the mid-nineteenth century, long before there was a Federal Reserve Bank to undertake the same role on behalf of government. The Suffolk Bank had done this very well for many years. It provided a very good practical case study for those who thought that private enterprise could in fact do many of the things that some thought lay only within the domain of government action.

The author was Professor George Trivoli, a US academic we had befriended through the Mont Pelerin and Philadelphia Societies. His factual empirical research on this private bank clearing system backed up some of the more theoretical findings of the Austrian School, an approach which mirrored our own. We, too, took the view that economics had to be about what economies and economic participants actually do, and had to be firmly grounded in the world of real experience.

Once again we did the artwork by hand and had the book printed by the firm that did *The Trojan Horse* for us. Like that publication it was done in hot metal, a very expensive process. The bill was a real struggle to pay (it took us months), and after that we went on to the newer printing technologies that used photographic or lithographic reproduction.

The book itself was modestly received, as it had to be, given its rather esoteric subject, but it did some important things. It proved of great interest to academics, and was still being cited three decades later. It also established the Adam Smith Institute as a body with an interest in scholarship and research, rather than one engaging in political advocacy or just policy recommendations. Academics, ever anxious to increase their range of publications, began to regard us as a possible outlet for their work, and numbers of them began to suggest lines of their research that we might be interested in publishing. It was another case of those unintended consequences that form such an important part of free-market literature.

Once again, without intending to set a precedent, we were doing things in a way that was to become one of our hallmarks. We continued to publish academic and theoretical works relating to our ideas, alongside the policy recommendations that attracted more interest in the media. We subsequently published Konrad Zweig's *Origins of the German Social Market Economy* and Thomas Taylor's *Fundamentals of Austrian Economics*, and continued this tradition throughout the Institute's existence.

We launched Konrad Zweig's book at a reception in the Alternative Bookshop, a libertarian bookseller set up by Chris Tame and Brian Mickelthwait of the Libertarian Alliance. This, while it lasted, served as a focus for libertarian and free-market activity, and was a great, if pokey, meeting place. Konrad Zweig's speech was not the best ever heard in the bookshop. In a very Germanic fashion he went through the book pointing out all the literal errors he wished to correct.

Our approach in all this was very much characterized by an empirical attitude. We were conscious of the fact that we did not really know what we were doing. How could we? We were heading into unexplored territory. We tried doing many different things and, if something worked, we did it again. We were never committed to doing things simply because that was what was expected, or what was normally done. If it did not work, we stopped doing it. And the fact that we had virtually no money was a powerful influence on us. It made us cost-effective because we had to be. It led us to devise novel and low-cost ways of achieving our objectives.

Obviously we had to limit our output to areas where we thought we might make a difference. We likened it to pushing on many doors simultaneously and, if we felt any give way a little, pushing harder on those. We never had the resources to squander on things that brought no results.

Along with *The Trojan Horse* and *The Suffolk Bank,* we published *More Effective Than Bombing*, by Stuart Butler. This was an examination of the impact of rent control and subsidized council housing upon the housing sector. Statutory rent controls severely restricted the supply of housing to let, while subsidized council housing, then accounting for 35 per cent of UK homes, limited mobility and restricted the market in housing. The piece strongly reinforced calls for the phasing out of rent controls on private accommodation, and for the sale of council homes to their tenants at discounted prices.

Milton Friedman, another prominent free marketeer and Nobel laureate, had made famous Carl Lindbeck's description of rent controls as 'the most effective means, short of bombing, of destroying a city'. We mischievously argued that they were more effective, in that bombing took out demand for housing as well as supply, giving us the title of our publication.

QUANGO, QUANGO, QUANGO

The publication that gave us greatest prominence in 1979 came a few months after *The Trojan Horse*. The backbench Tory MP, Philip Holland, had given assiduous attention to the rise of extra-parliamentary bodies which exercised powers outside parliamentary control. There were large and growing numbers of them, and they consumed a large and growing budget. They were the quasi-autonomous non-governmental organizations, or quangos.

There was no register of them, no public scrutiny and many of them had, in effect, the power to make regulation and even law without any debates in Parliament, much less the approval of Parliament. Philip Holland had tirelessly used Parliamentary Questions (PQs) to enquire of each minister in turn how many such public bodies came under their department, and how much they cost.

His definition of quangos, the one that came to be generally accepted, was non-departmental public bodies to which the minister had the power to make appointments of those other than civil servants or MPs. In practice they were bodies which had a role in the processes of government and which were funded by government, but which came outside government departments.

He had introduced the informed public to quangos with a 1978 Conservative Political Centre publication completed jointly with Michael Fallon, one of our St Andrews friends who was a parliamentary researcher at the time. Now it was time to bring these bodies to the notice of a wider public.

The Adam Smith Institute view was that such bodies should be brought under parliamentary scrutiny, their activities and budgets should be published, and ministers should be obliged to answer Parliamentary Questions concerning the quangos which came under their departments. Of course we also took the view that their explosive growth was undemocratic and that their numbers should be severely cut back. Our position towards them could be summed up as 'hostile'.

Holland's relentless probing had established that altogether there were 3,068 quangos, and that, while their budgets were not all available for inspection, their costs ran into hundreds of millions of pounds each year. Moreover they represented an insidious advance of technocratic, as opposed to democratic, government. They increased the scope for government by 'the great and the good' at the expense of the representatives of the people.

We took the decision to publish the list with a very short introductory essay and to do so in a way that would dramatize the problem that their growth represented. Eamonn suggested that we should publish them all on a single page. It was an idea we had seen done many years previously by Aims of Industry, listing all the nationalized ('publicly-owned') industries.

This posed a technical problem because the page would have to be over 12-feet long, but we solved this by sticking together several smaller pages and folding the 12-foot page so it fitted between the covers of a normal-size publication. The difference was that when this one was opened, the 12-foot page would unfold, dropping down from it. It was a gimmick, of course, but quite a dramatic one.

We called it *Quango, Quango, Quango*, in an allusion to the title of the once popular song, *Quando, Quando, Quando* (When, When, When), and we did the cover artwork ourselves, including the lettering. Again, we were setting two precedents that were to become our house style. Nearly all of our titles featured some play on words and for over two decades we prepared all the covers ourselves, painstakingly sticking down the letters from sheets of 'Letraset' instant lettering. This was dry transfer lettering sold in sheets of various typefaces and sizes. By rubbing down hard on the letters, they could be transferred onto artwork. It was a very fiddly operation that had to be done painstakingly, and the letter sheets did tend to degrade over time.

We had acquired skills like these up in St Andrews, and they enabled us to do the artwork ourselves at a fraction of the cost that professionals would have charged. We kept scrapbooks of drawings and designs we might want to use for future cut-and-paste cover designs. Only with the advent of personal computers and printers were we able to retire those skills.

We gave a great deal of thought to the press release. It had to be punchy and dramatic, and we had the advantage of having a popular and well-respected MP as our author. We spoke of 'the longest page in the world', though I doubt if it was. We listed the costliest quangos, the silliest, the most unnecessary and had a whole section on 'quite the quaintest quango' featuring some of the more bizarre ones. The *Hadrian's Wall Advisory Committee* attracted popular attention, though my personal favourite was the *Detergents and Allied Products Voluntary Notification Scheme Scrutiny Group*.

We went to meet Philip Holland on the Terrace of the Palace of Westminster and photographed him holding up the hugely long page, blowing in the wind. We sent out the photo with the press release and were gratified to see it appear on the front page of several national newspapers. We had told both the BBC and ITV, and the latter asked if they could preview the story on the evening before our embargo. They filmed the page rolling off the presses at our printers, with slightly self-conscious print workers looking on. 'The longest page in the world is unveiled tomorrow', was their story on the main 6 o'clock bulletin and *News at Ten*.

In a practice that would become common for us, we went down to Victoria Station after 11pm to pick up the first editions of the next day's papers. The coverage was massive: we were in all the national papers and most of the regionals. Quangos were put firmly onto the agenda of problems requiring action. Philip Holland had a leader page article on the subject in the *Daily Mail*, and the practice of running such pieces in the *Mail* on the day of publication became another of our regular practices.

One lesson we learned is that if there is popular unease about a development or trend, and we could tie a news story to it that put substance and numbers on to it, the media would eagerly cover it. Most of the papers not only ran the story of our publication, but wrote editorials on it denouncing the trend to secretive and unaccountable government. In a single day the Adam Smith Institute had become part of the background of policy analysis. We were simply there, just as if we had always been.

We continued with the quango story. Later that year we published, again by Philip Holland, *Costing the Quangos*, with the best analysis we could come up with as to how much these bodies cost the taxpayer each year. We followed it with *The Quango Death List*, picking out 707 of the quangos we thought most deserved the chop. It was a lightweight publication, but quite dramatic in appearance because Eamonn had designed a black cover with a white noose hanging down from the top. It was macabre enough to be attention-grabbing.

When the Conservatives won the 1979 election and Margaret Thatcher became Prime Minister, one of her early decisions was to undertake a thorough review of the quangocracy. She appointed a senior civil servant, Sir Leo Pliatzky, to examine the quangos and to make recommendations. Eamonn went to see him and came back describing him as 'very posh Oxford'. He told Eamonn that 'the Premster has charged me with solving this problem' and it took Eamonn some moments to figure out who the Premster might be.

Sir Leo duly reported that some of them should indeed be

culled, though his target list was only about 200 – a figure added to by Margaret Thatcher, who abolished 436 of them. More importantly, Sir Leo's reforms were implemented and brought quangos under parliamentary control. Ministers were obliged to publish details of their quangos, including their costs, and had to answer questions asked about them in Parliament.

It was a great boost for the ASI, since we had been seen to make the running with Philip Holland, and the campaign had led to government action. When we asked Sir Philip, as he later came to be titled, to write a definitive book about quangos, he at first declined, remarking, 'Oh, I could never write a book!' However, when we listed what the chapters might be, he began to see that each would be like a forty-minute speech, which he *could* write. When we eventually published it as *The Governance of Quangos*, we put a drawing on the cover of a capital 'Q' drawn as a vulture. Once again, it was a very striking cover. It gained even more coverage when Sir Philip casually told the media that he used to attract vultures when he was in Kenya. (He did it by lying spread-eagled on the ground, whereupon vultures would circulate above to see if he were in fact dead – it helped that he was cadaverously thin).

We continued the blitz on quangos by publishing a piece by Michael Fallon on *The Rise of the Euro-quango*, a publication which showed how Europe, too, had fallen into creating and funding large numbers of these off-government bodies which defied any kind of scrutiny, despite the huge costs they imposed upon European taxpayers. The rather smart cover we produced for it showed a Pac-man making its way through a maze while gobbling up currency.

In a later publication by Douglas Mason we also drew attention to the growth of similar bodies in UK local government, dubbing them 'qualgos'. All of these publications attracted considerable media attention, and placed the Institute firmly in the eye of public policy. At last it seemed that even though we were still tiny and had almost no money (though did have a huge overdraft and irritated printers calling up for payment), we had actually established some kind of presence. We were now, as we came to say, 'part of the woodwork'.

4

INSPECTORS

We kept up the pace of our publications despite being woefully under-funded. We did this by the simple device of producing very low-cost publications, doing the artwork ourselves, and sending camera-ready copy to the printers. Those years in St Andrews spent making up student publications with Letraset, an electric typewriter, Bostik glue and a 'process blue' pencil were serving us well. In one or two cases we published jointly with other organizations in order to split the production costs.

One such piece that attracted much attention was a survey of all of the different officials at national or local level who had the power to enter your home or business premises. This project was initiated by John Blundell, who had been a student friend from LSE and was now heading the National Federation of the Self-Employed (NFSE). We established that there were 201 different types of officer who could do this, and that they had at least 243 powers of actions the law allowed them to take. An Englishman's home was very far from being his castle.

There had been recent high-profile cases in which officials had taken part in dawn raids, holding children hostage in one room while they ransacked the premises on what were essentially fishing trips to see if they could discover anything incriminating. They were using statutory powers that went beyond and outside of the fundamental principles of English common law.

Once again with an eye to dramatizing the scale of this development, the book took the form of an introductory essay highlighting the menace, followed by a list of the inspectors and their powers, with a short entry on each of them. We formatted it like a restaurant guide, with symbols against each of the inspectors to depict the powers they could use. A flask denoted that they could take away samples, an axe meant that they could enforce entry, and so on. To add to the interesting quirkiness of the piece, we sought and obtained permission from a popular cartoonist to reproduce his cartoon of a policeman serving tea in bed to someone and being asked by the householder, 'This is your first dawn raid, isn't it?'

The powers themselves were far from amusing, though some were decidedly quirky. For example, the *Atomic Energy inspector* could enter your premises to see if you were dabbling in nuclear fission. My personal favourite was the fact that the *Ostrich and Fancy Feather and Artificial Flower Wages Council* could send in its inspectors to see if you were breaking their rules. Obviously these powers had been ceded out far too widely, leaving the homes and business premises vulnerable to a veritable army of snoopers, some armed with draconian powers.

I thought the obvious title for this study was *An Inspector Calls*, with an allusion to the celebrated play by J. B. Priestly. Eamonn was concerned that Priestly's estate might sue us for breach of copyright, so I reluctantly agreed to the alternative title, *An Inspector at the Door*. This was, incidentally, a demonstration of the fact that there was no hard and fast division of powers between the two directors of the Adam Smith Institute. In practice we never did anything unless we both agreed on it. We might try to persuade the other, but the default position was no action without agreement.

We were over-cautious because we did not understand laws relating to copyright or legal restrictions on what you could say in the public domain. With our limited resources we played safe. The report was therefore released as *An Inspector at the Door*, (published jointly with the NFSE) and received massive media coverage. The papers went to town and enjoyed highlighting some of the more outrageous and silly powers of entry that we had outlined in the report and helpfully set out in the press release that accompanied the publication. The *Ostrich and Fancy Feather and Artificial Flower Wages Council* had never had such widespread publicity though I doubt they enjoyed it.

Prime Minister Margaret Thatcher was asked in Parliament for her views on the Adam Smith Institute report, *An Inspector at the Door*. She replied, 'I have seen that report. It is a very valuable one. We must take it very seriously and look at it with a view to finding a means of reducing the numbers of occasions upon which inspectors can demand entry.' Her words came as a totally unexpected bonus.

Such an accolade was worth much to us because it made it clear that ideas have influence, and that our activities could indeed impact on events. She was as good as her word, too, and introduced measures to abolish the powers of thirty of these inspectors, and to reduce the powers of sixty-three others. It was another significant victory for us.

This turn of events also gave us the idea of using friendly MPs to put down Parliamentary Questions to draw the attention of other ministers to our reports. Sometimes, as on this occasion, they had done it without being asked, but we realized we could plan it as part of the campaign to put our ideas in the public domain. We referred to it colloquially as the 'nutcracker', because on the outside was our press publicity campaign to generate interest in the ideas, while on the inside a Parliamentary Question would draw it to the attention of the minister and the appropriate department and put it firmly into the political domain.

MEDIA FRIENDS

It helped very much in our early days to have people in the media who broadly shared our agenda. John O'Sullivan, writing for the *Telegraph* first, and then *The Times*, could usually contrive some reference to our latest publication, or induce one of his colleagues to cover it. He was one of a band of perhaps half a dozen such people we would meet socially and discuss how the campaign was going to transform Britain with free enterprise ideas and initiatives. Others who were supportive of us or interested in us included Derrick Hill, Peter Hennessy and Edward Pearce. Peter Hennessy had followed us with interest even during our student days, and was quite proud of the fact that he had 'discovered' us and given us our first national coverage.

Sir James Goldsmith's brand new weekly news magazine, *Now!*, a sort of glossy UK version of *Time* and *Newsweek*, was invaluable. He had recruited top journalists to write for it and had put substantial money behind it. While it never succeeded in attracting the mass circulation it would need to survive in the long term, it was read in detail by journalists from other papers and from the broadcast media. This meant that a story which played big in *Now!* magazine might well be picked up by daily papers or followed up by radio and TV interviewers.

Fortunately for the Adam Smith Institute, Sir James was very much on side. Having made his own fortune through his market talents, he favoured a society in which people of ability could themselves make good. Very charismatic, tall and with steely blue eyes, he had built himself a vast fortune through a series of controversial takeover deals that sought to wring value from under-performing companies.

He was a big supporter of the ASI, and had a very engaging way of showing it. Eamonn and I would be shown into his office to make our pitch. We were both complete novices at this, lacking any professional polish, but Sir James would listen courteously and attentively. He would ask a few shrewd questions, then announce with a beam that he approved of what we were doing and was going to support us. He would then call through on his intercom to have his secretary prepare a cheque, which he signed on the spot and handed to us as we left. We never had to wait for a decision to be sent on to us later; we walked out with the money.

His editor of *Now!* magazine, Anthony Shrimsley, was also a supporter and met us over lunch at L'Ecu de France, a place so expensive that our taxi driver flung his arms to full stretch and told us it cost that much 'just to get through the door'.

Tony contrived to run our stories whenever he could. We could occasionally allow *Now!* to have a story a day or so ahead of its release date, since the daily papers did not regard it as a direct competitor. When we released *An Inspector at the Door*, *Now!* carried a full page article about it by me, under the heading 'Society of Snoopers'. It helped the rest of the media to notice it.

This use of feature articles, which had started by chance with our first publication, *The Trojan Horse*, we now put into a system. It became our regular habit with a new publication to offer a national daily an exclusive article to publish on the day of release. It allowed the newspaper to make the story very topical by pointing out that the article was based on a paper 'published today by the Adam Smith Institute'.

More often than not it would be a feature page article in the *Daily Mail*. Its editor, Sir David English, was a superb editor with a fine intuition for what would work and what would not. With his features editor, Mac Keene, he would often suggest how the article might be developed, and what points might be covered in it. Pieces we authored in the *Daily Mail* included ones on tax self-assessment, reforming domestic and business rates, deregulation, privatizing the telephone service, quangos and Euro-quangos, and contracting out of local services, amongst many others.

All of this had the advantage – a major one – of paying money. The *Daily Mail* and *Now!* magazine paid particularly well, and a few hundred pounds for an article was a substantial sum for people working for an outfit that could not afford to pay them a salary.

Eamonn and I came up with a novel solution to the ASI's lack of funds and its inability to attract substantial financial backing (Sir James Goldsmith was one of a tiny number of contributors). We both secured part-time employment outside the Institute that left us enough time to run it. Once again, this was not something we set out to do, rather it was something we fell into out of necessity.

Eamonn was appointed editor of the *British Insurance Brokers Association* (BIBA) magazine. One of our St Andrews friends, Michael Forsyth, had set up a public relations company that had successfully bid to run a magazine for the BIBA members. There was a budget, as well as advertising revenue, and this was sufficient to meet the salary of a part-time editor. Michael asked Eamonn to step into the role, knowing he would be good at it having seen him edit several St Andrews magazines while they were students there.

For several years Eamonn served in this role. It was not too demanding, and it had the side effect of giving him considerable knowledge and expertise about the way in which the financial industry operated, as well as a significant number of contacts in the business. I had a rather fun role of selecting the winner of the monthly caption competition.

My own part-time work was as relief leader writer for the *Daily Mail*. They had two full-time leader writers, and their practice was to have one of them write all the editorials, usually three, for the day. Rather than have someone do this every day, their policy was to have one person write them for five days, with the other one doing the sixth day. The next week it would be the other way round. This was an efficient system, and Chris Nicholson and Russell Lewis did it very well. The problem came when one of them went on holiday or if one of them took ill. This was why they needed a relief leader writer to come in on such days.

I did not apply for the post, or even know of its existence. The *Mail* had lost their previous relief and needed a replacement. Apparently Sir David had been hard to please and this had gone on for weeks. Then Russell Lewis suggested my name and, when Sir David acquiesced having seen several of my articles in his paper, they confirmed the appointment with alacrity.

I only did it for perhaps two days or so a month, but it paid well, and gave me a very good working knowledge of how the press functioned, with its priorities and deadlines. It made the ASI more effective in its own relationship with the media. I found it easy to relate to the other journalists, although they regarded leader-writers as somewhat other-worldly, detached from the pressures of news deadlines and exclusives. This was enhanced by the fact that I wore bow ties, as I had done since boyhood. Since the other two leader writers were also bow-tie wearers, the newsroom staff formed the view that this was a sort of uniform.

The bow ties became almost a trademark for the ASI, though I only ever wore them when I was on show or when smart dress was required.

CONTRACTING OUT

While the weaknesses of public sector supply were quite well known and documented, analysts disagreed about how they should be redressed. Public services often enjoyed a monopoly position and had access to taxpayer funds without the need to attract customers. There was even Crown immunity, meaning that there was no legal redress over large parts of the public sector. They tended to be inefficient and over-priced, as well as under-capitalized and out of date in their practices. In the absence of competition or consumer pressure, they tended towards producer capture, serving the interests of their political masters, their administrators and their workforce, instead of those of the public at large.

Some commentators supposed that they needed to charge for their services as an alternative to direct public funding. Arthur Seldon, the formidably 'dry' editor at the IEA had written a book on the subject. Unfortunately charging for services has political weaknesses because legislators are reluctant to keep prices at economic levels when this incurs the wrath of their electors. There are often public outcries when prices are raised to take account of rising costs.

Some Conservatives favoured a technocratic approach, putting strong managers into the civil service to impose techniques such as those found routinely in private sector businesses. The problem with this approach is that will-power only goes so far, and lasts only so long, when there are not the pressures in place which force private businesses to stay lean and efficient.

Our approach was different. We came to the conclusion that only real competition would produce those pressures and therefore favoured the use of private contractors, rather than public service employees, to deliver public services. And even if public authorities decided to keep their own service departments, we suggested they should still face competition from private providers to keep them on their toes.

We scoured the world for examples and came up with many. Rubbish collection was routinely handed to private contractors in many US cities. Some used contractors for street cleaning. Scottsdale in Arizona had hired a private fire service. In Denmark much ambulance work was carried out by the private Falck company.

We collected the facts, figures and the results, and gradually built up a powerful, indeed overwhelming, case for using private firms to bid for and carry out local authority works, based entirely on practical experience in other countries, rather than on some theoretical model. Michael Forsyth had now added the role of local councillor to his other activities, and was very willing to be the author of our report making the case for this to be done in Britain.

The US Reason Foundation had done good work in this area, and readily provided us with many examples and US success stories. We called the paper *Reservicing Britain* and prepared to publish it. Although it was, in effect, a pamphlet in its format, we made it our policy never to use the word 'pamphlet' in any of our releases. 'Pamphlets' conjured up the idea of small, lightweight political tracts urging a point of view. We wanted our publications to be regarded differently, so we called them 'studies', 'papers', 'reports', and other euphemisms. The emphasis we sought was on researched ideas backed up by empirical examples and data.

We had taken photographs of the mountains of black refuse bags filling Leicester Square during the 'Winter of Discontent' disputes, and now used one of these as the cover photograph for our publication. It gave it quite a striking appearance. When it was ready, Michael used his PR skills to give it a good send-off. In addition to our usual style of press release, he used his firm's personnel and resources to back its release.

A launch party was organized within the House of Commons itself and Michael contrived to bring in Lord Bellwin, the local government minister, plus several high-ranking Tories. We invited some of our friends, including Rhodes Boyson, the ex-headteacher turned MP, now acknowledged as a rising star. The media was there in force, with some of our more cynical friends saying it was for the free drink, available in copious quantities. The press spotted the senior Tory figures turning up for the launch of the publication and treated it as politically significant. Lord Bellwin made a speech wholeheartedly welcoming the report and praising its innovative approach as one that held great promise for local government throughout Britain.

The message was clear: government was going to make it happen. In fact a few Conservative-controlled local authorities such as Wandsworth decided not to wait for government help, but to do it anyway and gain the glory given to pioneers and trail-blazers.

The Prime Minister enthusiastically supported the policy. We were told by her Downing Street team that she had ordered 20,000 photo-copies of *Reservicing Britain* so that one could be sent to every Conservative councillor all over Britain. We were sufficiently flattered that we decided not to press charges for the breach of our copyright. The entire print run sold out almost immediately, so we ran a second edition in much larger quantities with an even more striking cover in red and black, but using the same photograph of the refuse bags.

Michael Forsyth arranged a slide show presenting the idea to show at a Conservative local government conference in London, arousing even more interest in the proposal. He used a variety of PR presentational skills to boost the idea at every turn. It took about six to nine months, perhaps, to turn the tide against in-house public service provision at local level, and towards the use of competitive tendering. Ironically, councils gained more control over the private contractors than they had ever had over their own employees and their unions.

Overnight, the effort turned the ASI into authorities on local government contracting, and we found our postbox stuffed with invitations to speak on the subject. There was a general perception that something new and exciting was being said. We declined most of the invitations because of the travel time involved but decided to organize our own conferences on the subject, inviting local authorities to send delegates to learn the ins and outs of using contractors, and the lessons to be learned.

The first of these took place in the Whitbread Brewery conference room, leading one of our speakers, Sir John Grugeon from Kent County Council, to announce that we could indeed organize a rave-up in a brewery. It caused some difficulty for the six councillors and officials who attended from Blaenau Gwent. Since it coincided with the Christmas shopping period, their local press denounced it as 'junketing'. But it worked, and it made money for us. Its speeches even gave us the chapters of a publication, *Economy and Local Government*.

Reservicing Britain was the first of many publications the ASI released in the subject, and we rapidly learned from the practical experience of pioneering local authorities which were the best practices to follow. The government followed through on its support for the idea, eventually introducing a Bill that required local authorities to put large parts of their work out to competitive tender.

We learned from this exercise just how much we did not know about promoting our ideas. We picked up from the PR industry how to involve high-profile figures and how to organize meetings that could command the attention of those we wanted to reach.

While taking part in a televised debate on the subject for Anglia Television, we won over most of the audience by simply asking for the idea to be tried out. Our research had made us confident that putting out local services to competitive tender would generate such positive results in terms of both price and quality that others would soon follow the example of the pioneers.

We discovered that the general public is sufficiently fair-minded to go along with the notion of testing new ideas on a limited basis, and we often thereafter called for many of our proposals to be introduced on an experimental basis in a few trial areas to see how they performed in practice before being rolled out nationally. It was a discovery that was to echo through much of our subsequent work.

FREEPORTS

This affected the way in which we campaigned for the introduction of freeports within Britain. To some extent our proposal was a response to the lacklustre performance of Enterprise Zones. Great things had been touted of enterprise zones, proposed originally by Professor Sir Peter Hall of Reading, but when it came to implementing the idea, the civil service had shown considerable reluctance to relinquish control. This was especially true of the Treasury, which was in no mood to have some parts of the country subject to lower taxes and regulations.

Enterprise zones had originally been conceived as a way of allowing relatively unfettered free enterprise to stimulate economic growth and revitalize under-performing areas of the country. As applied in practice, the advantages they were supposed to offer were very limited. It was another lesson in Public Choice; the bureaucracy was reluctant to surrender control.

Planning was made easier in some cases and there were modest financial incentives, of which the most significant was a ten-year relief from local business rates. Eleven such areas were designated originally, followed by a further thirteen. But by now they resembled not 'enterprize zones', but 'subsidy islands'.

It was obvious from the outset that they were unlikely to achieve what had originally been expected of them. Indeed, a later study found that between them they had created only 13,000 net new jobs despite costing nearly £300m. Only the enterprise zone in Canary Wharf could perhaps be judged an unqualified success, and that had other advantages, chief among which was its proximity to London's financial district, where there was such pressure for space. The powerful support this one enjoyed from Trade Minister Michael Heseltine was also a factor.

We decided to try a different tack, with the aim of showing just what free enterprise could achieve if it were set free from many of the restrictions and costs imposed upon it by government. The idea was to have a few test areas of limited size to highlight the contrast between the growth they would create versus that achieved in other areas not so designated.

We undertook a study of freeports around the world and concluded that they could provide another chance to test the principle in Britain. Freeports are basically areas within a country which are treated as if they are outside tax jurisdiction. Goods brought into them do not incur customs or tariffs until they leave the freeport, and not even then if they are sent abroad. There are two types of freeport: those in which imports are simply stored until they are trans-shipped, and those which manufacture and add value to imported goods within the freeport before they are exported from it. It is the second type of freeport which grows businesses and creates jobs, and this is the type we advocated.

It would be especially applicable as a possible way to revive run-down dock areas of the country which had seen their trade shrivel over the years. We published a short proposal outlining the idea, then organized a conference at Windsor Castle featuring experts in the field.

In another move that came to typify our house style, we turned the conference papers into the chapters of a book we could publish on the subject. We had done this already on the use of private contractors to perform local services; now we did it for freeports. This gave us three bites at the cherry in fairly short order: the proposal, the conference and the report.

The Treasury had always opposed freeports, fearing the loss of a revenue stream if they were used to slip goods out of reach of customs and excise duties. A Treasury official even told one of our authors privately that there were 'several shelves' in the Treasury filled with their past successes in fending off the idea.

We advocated that a small number of freeports, perhaps six, should be established, and the material was sent out to local newspapers across the country. It was taken up enthusiastically at a local level, with communities clamouring to be considered for freeport status as a means of boosting jobs and regenerating derelict areas.

We had the ear of the Department of Trade and Industry, if not the Treasury. The DTI became enthusiasts for the idea and were quite happy to have their ministers express public support for it. The Secretary of State, Cecil Parkinson, was a valuable and eloquent supporter of the idea, and helped the campaign to gain its adoption. The momentum for the proposal built up as more and more local authorities indicated their desire to have a freeport in their area. Together with support from Cabinet members who generally favoured free enterprise policies, it created a formidable coalition in favour.

A ministerial working party was set up to study the idea and report on it. It included Iain Sproat, the Under-Secretary at Trade and Industry, and a keen supporter of the idea. He was aviation minister and liked the idea of freeports next to airports, as in Miami. His working party recommended in favour of freeports being established within the UK.

When the Prime Minister came on side, the Treasury had to concede on the principle of freeports, but concentrated instead on restricting the concessions which would apply within them. The government announced its intention to establish six freeports and invited local authorities to bid. Different communities prepared their bids, generating vast amounts of local press coverage. Eventually nearly four dozen places entered bids to be one of the six chosen.

The general election of 1983 came between the announcement, the invitation to bid and the actual decision as to which were to be the successful six. The ones finally designated as British freeports were Humberside, Liverpool, Prestwick, Sheerness, Southampton and Tilbury. Significantly five of them were maritime ports and one was adjacent to an airport.

By this time it was clear that the ASI's radical proposal had been watered down, as usual, into something that would make very few waves. Indeed, the only substantial concession was that goods would be exempt from customs duty and VAT while in the freeports. No other taxes or regulations were waived, so the main assistance to businesses using the freeports was help with their cash flow, in that they did not have to pay the taxes up front.

This was not what we had in mind when we originally proposed that freeports be established in Britain. We wanted, as we had with enterprise zones, to reduce the burden of taxation and regulation in selected areas in order to show what kind of growth free enterprise might achieve if government sat more lightly upon its shoulders. The civil service, on the other hand, did not want that to happen and feared that if such zones were set up they would risk seeing some of their potential tax base diminish as businesses set up within these zones, or transferred into them.

Although we were successful in having the idea for British free-ports adopted, with six of them established we did not regard the outcome as a success. They were of limited value in the guise in which they were established, and came nowhere near achieving any of the goals we had hoped for.

THE ASI INDEX

During our time on Capitol Hill, both Eamonn and I had been impressed by the way in which legislators in Congress and the Senate were assessed on their voting record. Several organizations regularly published tables which listed representatives according to how they had voted on particular issues. The American Civil Liberties Union (ACLU), for example, ranked representatives on how they had voted on issues which the ACLU thought had bearing on the civil liberties Americans enjoyed. Similarly there were Conservative organizations which assessed how conservative or liberal each representative was, based on their voting record.

There were many of these so-called 'ratings'. Some were absurdly partisan, such as the one drawn up by teachers' unions that declared people in Congress and the Senate to be 'anti-education' if they had opposed forced bussing of children to achieve racial quotas in high schools. Others had more credibility, however, and were reckoned to be useful in assessing where representatives stood on the political spectrum, and how they were likely to vote on upcoming issues. It indicated to lobbyists who might be open to argument and therefore worth targeting on individual issues.

We wondered if a similar exercise could be done in Britain.

The key difference lay in the US separation of powers. In the US the executive, wielding presidential powers, was separate from the legislature which made the laws. In Britain, however, the executive was formed from those who enjoyed a majority within the legislature. Furthermore, the whipping of parliamentary votes in the UK was both routine and disciplined, whereas it was an altogether looser thing in the US Houses of Congress. MPs in Britain were normally required to vote along party lines, whereas in the US it was left to the conscience of the individual legislator.

These were formidable obstacles, but we thought there might be ways round them. Some parliamentary votes were deemed to be 'issues of conscience' and not subject to party whipping. Sometimes there were rebellions against the party line on particular issues, some of them quite widespread. We looked at the votes which had taken place during the parliamentary session, picking out only those where party whipping had been absent or where rebellions against the party line had been sufficiently large to mean that whipping had been ineffective on those occasions. The whips might threaten to discipline one or two MPs to bully them into line, but there was no way this could work with dozens of them.

The issue we wanted to focus upon was whether the MPs voted in ways that extended choices for the individual citizen or in ways that augmented the area in which the state made the choices. In addition to votes which were obviously on matters relating to personal freedom, we took votes for increased taxes and spending to be ones which diminished the choices of how people might spend their own money and increased the ability of the state to take those decisions instead.

One of the Conservative students, Mark Loveday, volunteered to do the work on the project, and painstakingly went through Hansard listing how each MP had voted, and which divisions could count as either free votes or ineffectively whipped ones and which subjects bore on personal liberty issues. In those pre-computer days this was quite a laborious exercise.

We found there were just enough such votes during the first year of the new (post-1979) parliament to form a reasonable basis for rating MPs according to whether they favoured individual choices and decisions or state action instead. We duly published the ASI Index, with an explanatory chapter explaining our purpose and methodology.

Somewhat to our surprise the press was very interested and gave prominence to the high and low scorers. Lincolnshire MPs Michael Brotherton and Michael Brown were feted as top scorers in the liberty index. Local newspapers in particular covered the performance of the MPs representing constituencies in their own area. The exercise yielded many column inches, and put across our central point that personal liberty mattered and that an MP's stand on issues involving liberty was a reasonable way to highlight their philosophical stance.

In emphasizing personal liberty, the index also highlighted the fact that the ASI was libertarian rather than paternalistic or authoritarian. It separated us to some extent from the traditional Tory right wing. We published the index two years in a row, and in the second included an appendix pull-out chart which featured all the MPs as dots on a graph. The horizontal scale represented choice on economic issues, while the vertical scale covered social and civil issues. Each MP had two numbers, showing how they had scored on each scale.

MPs tended to cluster fairly consistently. The Tories (in blue) were mostly in positive territory on economic freedoms, but much less so on the social scale. Labour MPs (in red) scored low on economic choice, but rather higher on the social freedoms. The press was quite interested in the outriders, especially the few Tories who scored high on both scales, which was the position roughly representing where we stood ourselves.

Quite unexpected was the keen interest the exercise attracted from some university politics and political science departments. They took it to be a serious presentation of useful data. Several academics started to follow the ASI's work and some began coming to our conferences, and in some cases participating in them. A few later contributed papers which we published.

We were not surprised by some of the hostile comments we attracted from MPs who came down low in our ratings. They did not like the implication that they were opposed to personal liberties and choices, even though some of them patently were. Some of them had strongly held convictions on issues such as abortion and gay rights, and opposed any liberalization measures, On the ASI Index, these counted as votes against individual choice and some of those who scored low resented that.

On the other hand, some of the high-scoring MPs trumpeted their high scores, adding to their parliamentary biographies the fact that they had been among the group at the top of the ASI Parliamentary Index. Some who were not already our friends became so as a result of the exercise. Useful though the activity had been, we decided that it consumed too much of our time and resources to justify its continuation. There were other, more pressing matters that called for our attention.

5

YOUTH OUTREACH

From its very beginning, the Adam Smith Institute always had good links with young people in schools and university. We had only recently left university ourselves and still had many contacts with friends we had made there. The summer *Open Society* symposium attracted many current students each year, while our summer programmes for US students brought us into contact with others, and crucially with university staff.

Having no money to pay staff, we often recruited student helpers to assist us with the organization of conferences, seminars and press receptions. They would do it basically for pocket money and their enthusiasm for the causes of freedom and free markets.

The effect of all this was to make the Adam Smith Institute look very young. Many political meetings featured middle-aged or elderly audiences, whereas ours were always full of young people. It made the meetings brighter and more lively, so what had started more or less accidentally became policy.

Universities and schools are often on the lookout for speakers to address their societies, so we accepted as many as we could fit in. This occasionally involved long train journeys, but we could always fit in some work on the train, writing or editing. Typically we kept speeches short, down to perhaps twenty minutes, leaving plenty of time for questions and discussion. It had the benefit of keeping us in tune with what young people were thinking, and what issues concerned them. We could address their agenda instead of trying to foist another one on them.

Another factor that made it easy for us to develop a following among young people was that we were fairly tolerant and not judgemental in our attitudes to them. That, in itself, arose partly from our libertarian outlook that recognized peoples' right to make their own choices and do things their own way. Added to that was the fact that we were presenting a very radical programme. In a clean break from the centre-left consensus that had brought Britain so low, we offered the vision of a brighter tomorrow, one in which people would take more responsibility for their lives and find more opportunities for advancement. We had an intellectually consistent philosophy and a programme that could give effect to it. This combination was one that young people were attracted to.

It was not, however, one that all young people favoured. The battle for the soul of the Conservative Party was reflected in its youth echelons, and was perhaps more divisive and bitterly contested than in the senior party. Young people within the Conservative Party who supported free markets and fairly libertarian ideas were opposed by those still committed to the centre-left consensus, and supportive of the state's role as manager of the economy.

Those on the left, the so-called 'wets', were gradually losing support among the Conservative students and in the Young Conservatives, but they were well funded, and centred around the Tory Reform Group. They had powerful party figures ready to back them, including Peter Walker. They retained a loyalty to Edward Heath and a disdain for Margaret Thatcher, together with her polices and supporters. They favoured working within the National Union of Students, rather than denying it credibility and working to disaffiliate from it.

Against them, the reformers seeking free-market policies could count on the goodwill of the centre-right think tanks, including the Adam Smith Institute. They called themselves 'dries', and began flocking to our seminars and conferences, and using ASI-branded goods to denote their allegiance. They invited us to speak at their universities and to write articles in their magazines. The free-market students at our meetings were less likely to show the 'Tory boy' look of suits and ties, and tended to sport a funky, fashionable look. Some wore Adam Smith ties through their belt loops, knotted to hold up their jeans.

There was an element of personal ambition in this dispute, in that many of the participants envisaged a political career at some stage, and thought it important that they and their friends should be in control of the Conservative Party and its institutions in order to advance their own prospects. This was more true of those on the left, in that they lacked the binding presence of an underlying philosophy to unite their ideas, and emphasized instead the importance of good management of the economy and society, rather than following the set of principles which should underlie it.

There was a third group in Conservative student politics, those who followed the traditional agenda of the party's right wing. They had no time for libertarian ideas and favoured a more authoritarian outlook to shape society as they thought it should be. Their policies included tough stances on crime and immigration, and a more overt patriotism. For some reason we never discovered this group was termed the 'shits', as opposed to the 'wets' and the 'dries'. All three factions would fight for power and office within the Conservative students and the Young Conservatives.

The fight was protracted and bitter, continuing for several years. All three groups, but especially the 'wets', would stop at nothing to discredit their opponents, and would attempt to plant hostile stories in the press or to brief against their opponents. One of them collected a dossier of scurrilous stories that he himself had planted over the years, and used that dossier as 'evidence' of how harmful the 'dries' were! His fabrications resulted in several legal actions in which the newspapers that had fallen for his plants had to pay substantial damages in out-of-court settlements.

The Adam Smith Institute served as a kind of beacon to the 'dries': our proposals fitted with their own philosophical outlook, and our high media profile and readiness to argue the case for markets, incentives and privatization, seemed more attractive than talk of more efficient management of the state sector. The ones who lived out of London would come to visit us when they were in town and would pick up copies of our publications to circulate back in their universities.

We did not charge students for our publications or places at our seminars and conferences, remembering our own impoverished student days. Over the course of a couple of years the libertarian free-market students gradually assumed a dominance within the Federation of Conservative Students (FCS) and provided vocal backing for the Thatcherite policies which the Conservative government was adopting, and which were vehemently opposed by the hard-left elements who seemed dominant within the National Union of Students (NUS).

THE BOOK

While at St Andrews, I had written and circulated a short series of paragraphs to refute many of the common errors put about by the left. I wrote them on the back page of our newsletter MIDAS.

The first was called *Nine Lies about Capitalism*, followed by *Nine Truths about Socialism*, and then *Nine Facts about Freedom*. They were written in a punchy style and combatively worded. Taken together they amounted to a defence of freedom and capitalism and a repudiation of collectivism and statism.

Some of our student friends and allies had read them and asked whether the ASI might produce a short up-to-date guide for students, listing all the arguments used by the left and explaining in very brief terms exactly why they were wrong. They thought it would be useful for right-minded students to have access to such a brief at student union meetings, debates and conferences.

I reworked and updated some of the material I had written at St Andrews, covering all of the major themes the left regularly came out with. They were things like 'business oppresses the poor', or 'capitalism in based on greed', and included treatment of developing countries and the record of socialist ones. The aim was to correct the myths that business cheats its workers and its customers, and to show in terse terms how it benefits them and improves their living standards. I came up with 101 such arguments, and provided the counter-argument usually in a single paragraph of explanation.

The book was published in a plain, sombre black cover, with just the small white lettering of the title *the book* written in the lower case chancery script of my own handwriting on the front and the spine. There was no author listed, just a quotation from Orwell's *Nineteen Eighty-Four* on the flyleaf:

> …there were also whispered stories of a terrible book, a compendium of all the heresies … which circulated clandestinely here and there. It was a book without a title. People referred to it, if at all, simply as the book.

To add to the mystique of *the book* it was circulated in a clandestine fashion, like the one in Orwell's story. It was never advertised and could not be bought. Instead it was handed out surreptitiously, sometimes left in a student's room or slipped under their door. Occasionally it was passed on folded inside a newspaper at a students' union meeting. It was both slim and narrow, having been designed to fit into the back pocket of a pair of jeans so students could take it with them to meetings.

The aim was to give it an air of mystery and the feeling to those who read it that they were insiders, party to some secret cause. Some students produced badges to wear, simply declaring 'I've read *the book*'. There were a few small newspaper stories about it, speculating on its possible origins. The hope in circulating it was that it would impart both confidence and conviction to students that, although the left might be in a majority at most universities, they were not in the right.

There was a postscript to this story many years later. I would occasionally meet people who had encountered it while they were students and who spoke appreciatively of it. I sometimes thought of updating and reissuing it, but never did anything about it. Then I began giving a series of lectures to schools entitled 'Ten Things That Everybody Gets Wrong', similarly listing and refuting common errors of economics or social comment. Some of the students asked if I would write them up so they could have the arguments in condensed form.

I began by writing them one at a time on the ASI blog. Because we try to keep entries on that site down to a screen page or less, the word limit is about 360 words. As I did more of them, I found myself drawing on the list I had originally done for *the book*. After I had done maybe two or three dozen of them, I sought help from the ASI staff and the leading lights in The Next Generation (the

ASI's youth group) to extend the list to 101 again. A full list gradually took shape.

We decided part way through that the entries could be put together to make a book, somewhat in the style of the original. The list had to be considerably updated since by this time the Soviet Union and its communist governments had long collapsed, and there were new environmental fallacies and nonsenses being put about that cried out to be exposed. It was also reassuringly true that twenty-five years after the original appeared, very few people now argued that socialist organization of the economy and society was more efficient that its market counterpart.

Deleting quite a few of the old errors and highlighting new ones that had replaced them in the left's arsenal, I reached 101, putting one a day on the blog. This meant that the whole lot took just over three months to complete. It was published in 2007 as *Freedom 101,* a reference to the numbering of US university courses.

There was no attempt, or any need, for viral marketing this time. This book had both a title and my name on it as author. It was made available from the ASI and from Amazon, and soon clocked up a much larger circulation than *the book* had ever done, though it was not as much fun to be involved in.

SABBATICALS, INTERNS AND GAP YEARS

The volume of work at the ASI was becoming more than Eamonn and I could manage, but there was no way we could afford to employ someone. We were not paying ourselves, but even a relatively junior secretary in London commanded a salary beyond our reach, plus National Insurance and all the paperwork and complexity involved in deducting PAYE income tax.

The thought occurred to us that we might take on a student, someone taking a year out of university to acquire experience that might help them in a politics or economics degree. This was not like a gap year between school and university. We were thinking of something more like the sabbatical year awarded sometimes to students who were elected as Students' Union President or some other local or national administrative post. Typically this would pay approximately what it took to sustain a student for a year at university, which was considerably less than the starting salary of a job in London.

We put the idea to our student friends and were pleased when they gave it instant and enthusiastic support. They told us that such a post would be regarded as a plum job in student circles. We discussed the cost and worked out we could just about meet it, given there would be no income tax or National Insurance to bother with. The main problem would be finding space in the London flat for the appointee to work at. We needed another desk and somewhere to put it.

A candidate was suggested to us, a Dundee student named David Boyd, who was active in FCS and keen to spend a year in London with the ASI before finishing his degree. He seemed highly suitable, motivated and quick to learn. He stayed with us for a year and his soft Scottish accent stayed with us for years afterwards as the outgoing voice on our message machine. When David used to visit us, as he did for years afterwards, he would leap instinctively from his seat to answer the doorbell whenever it rang.

This gap-year employment began a practice that was to characterize the Adam Smith Institute for many years afterwards. We employed a student, either taking a year out from their university course, or wanting to spend a year working with us after graduating and before moving on to a job in London. It gave the ASI a youthful look to have students and their friends milling about.

Some of our friends used to joke that the ASI consisted of 'two men and a dog, but without the dog'. Now for a few years the ASI became three people, with the two directors and a student making up the entire complement. After that we began to appoint two student sabbatical year people and, later still, a part-time secretary. But by that time we needed an office.

THE ASI OFFICE

For its first few years the Institute did not have a separate office. Eamonn and I had bedrooms at opposite ends of the flat we had leased and used the space in between as the ASI offices. It actually worked surprisingly well, and we even used it to meet people there, but it did put limitations on what we could do. We fell into the habit of meeting most people outside at local cafés or over lunch.

While we usually went into studios to do radio and TV slots, producers occasionally wanted location shots, and it took a great deal of time and space to set up a TV interview in the flat. At one stage we even made a folding notice board covered with ASI material and press coverage so we could be filmed with it behind us in a hotel room or studio, turning it into a kind of 'instant ASI'.

When we moved to having two students instead of one, the need for office space became pressing. The problem was that we needed to be in Westminster where office space was very expensive. We found an interim solution, however. The building that later became the Department for Education was being completely made over by Land Securities, but they had to wait until the last remaining tenants had served out their leases before they could send in the builders.

Since they were modest supporters of the ASI, we asked them nicely if they would let us occupy one of the now-vacant offices until they had the rest of the building empty. They agreed to let us have one long office room entered from Abbey Orchard Street and charged us a fairly modest rent, given that we had agreed to move out whenever they wanted us to.

We bought more book shelving and used it to make two huge bookcases that effectively divided the space into three small, inter-connected office rooms. In those pre-internet days we needed to keep a large stock of publications to send out in packets when people ordered them.

We persuaded the phone company to give us a landline exten-sion all the way to the flat, so anyone calling the ASI would be answered first at the Abbey Orchard Street offices by our student sabbatical employees, and then put through to me or Eamonn at the flat if they needed to speak to us.

The two of us continued to work from the flat, leaving the students to run the office. It is a practice that has continued throughout the ASI's history. The young employees have the office to themselves without the ever-present supervision of the two directors. This has allowed us more peace and quiet to think and work without the ever-present interruptions of telephone calls or visitors. And it has given the young staff more independence than they would be awarded at most other establishments.

The Abbey Orchard Street offices worked very well. They were only a few hundred yards round the corner from the flat, so we could all readily travel between the two buildings. They gave us the luxury of space. We still had the smallest office space of any think tank, as well as the smallest staff and the smallest budget, but we could now hold business meetings and events in reasonably presentable offices. We even held evening receptions there, and for days afterwards would find wine glasses resting on our bookcases.

We were at the Abbey Orchard Street offices for three years before Land Securities needed their building back and we had to leave. Fortunately another office became available at just the right time. The coin dealer Vecchio's had operated from 23 Great Smith Street, a part of Church House owned by the Church of England and leased out commercially. Now Vecchio's staff had decided to return to Italy, leaving the premises vacant.

It was ideal for us, being about the size we needed and at a rent we could just about afford. Furthermore, it was even closer to the flat than the Abbey Orchard offices had been, about half the distance away. We approached the Church Commissioners and put in a request for the lease. We were successful, largely because we had asked at just the right time, were ready to move in straight away and did not pose any problems with our proposed use of it. A popular shop with a stream of customers, or a business that created smell or noise, would have been less satisfactory from their point of view. We would be quiet and not create any kind of nuisance.

We wondered if our public stance in favour of markets and personal liberties might cause the Church Commissioners some problems, but apparently it did not. In any case, as Eamonn pointed out, the huge Italian Restaurant in their basement had operated for many years under the name of *Vitello d'Oro*, which translated as 'The Golden Calf'. This did not seem to cause Church House any problems either, though they did have an internal discussion about it.

An address in Great Smith Street was also a happy coincidence for the Adam Smith Institute, with some people assuming that it had been named after Adam Smith himself. In fact the land had been bought by the Church from one Henry Smith in 1711, and the names Great Smith Street, Little Smith Street and even Smith Square seem to derive from that. Abbey Orchard Street had enjoyed a more interesting history, having been where Westminster Abbey's fruit trees once were.

As an office, our new place was small, with just a single room and two tiny store rooms. It had a small sink and a toilet, though, and the room was a more useful shape than our Abbey Orchard Street one had been. There was room for three office desks and, with judicious spacing, we could manage a floor area big enough to hold receptions for fifty people or more.

The Adam Smith Institute has been at its Great Smith Street office ever since. Most visitors are surprised by how small the Institute is. Many of them seem to imagine that the ASI resides on several floors of some luxury office block, with busy secretaries flitting backwards and forwards. The reality has always been a more modest one, with a small office and a handful of very young employees.

THE NEXT GENERATION

The young people who involved themselves in the activities of the ASI were a loose collection of friends and supporters until one of them, a boy called Sheldon Wilkie, suggested that we should organize regular activities specifically for young people. It struck a chord with us, and we began holding monthly receptions for the sixteen to thirty age group. We called the group 'The Next Generation' after the new *Star Trek* series using that name. We served a chosen 'wine of the month' and canapés, deliberately trying to make it look more up-market than the more common Coke or beer and sandwiches featured at other youth groups.

We sent out taster's notes about the wine with our snazzy invitation cards and invited speakers to give a ten-minute address in the middle. We usually met on the first Tuesday of the month so that our guests would know to mark off the date.

The numbers soon built up to the point where we could expect seventy or so to turn up. Guest speakers spread the word that The

Next Generation were the brightest and best youngsters around. They were certainly the liveliest, quite unlike the more sober-suited and subdued young people at most Westminster functions.

Over the years The Next Generation receptions developed into one of the ASI's best activities. Literally hundreds of young people came through our doors to meet each other and our guest speakers. We never advertised or sought to recruit members of the group; they simply came to our door.

6

PRIVATIZATION AND *STRATEGY TWO*

The manifesto on which the first Thatcher administration had gained office was a relatively modest affair. It did not mention privatization, although it talked of returning certain industries such as British Aerospace to the private sector. However, over time the word itself began to be used and was taken to mean having activities which had been performed in the public sector done instead in the private sector.

This could be done in a variety of ways. We initially identified seventeen different ways in which it could take place. For example, the public service itself might be ring-fenced, turned into a corporation, then sold, either to a private buyer or buyers, or to its management and employees, or to the general public by a share issue. It might be wholly sold, or the whole of it might be partly sold, with the government retaining a residual share. Under Treasury rules, if that holding fell below 50 per cent, the company was treated as private, and no longer had to appear on the list of government-owned assets.

We used the word privatization to describe all of these, and a variety of other techniques, including the use of private contractors to perform services that had previously been done 'in house' by government departments. The word itself increasingly made its appearance in the world of public policy. We certainly did not invent the word, nor ever claimed to.

We read in one paper that the word had been in use in Australia in the 1930s, long before any of us were born. We embraced its use and always spelled it with the 'z' instead of the 's', which can be an alternative spelling in English, but not in American English. We chose to spell it with a 'z' because it made it look newer. Some purists did not like the word and clamoured for 'denationalization' to be used instead, as it was more familiar. Others, allegedly including Margaret Thatcher, thought the word itself was ugly. One MP objected to the Americanization (which he spelled with an 's'), so we sent him information that the Oxford English Dictionary and *The Times* style guide both gave the 'z' endings as preferred.

But denationalization referred to the process by which Conservative governments had reversed some of the state ownership implemented by previous Labour governments. Some of them, such as steel, had been taken in and out of the state sector like yo-yos. The word suggested returning them to their previous owners. This was not the policy we were referring to. The talk now was of placing in the private sector some activities that had never been there before, and putting them into the hands of completely new owners, often the general public. The use of 'denationalization' implied the reversal of a previous policy, a going back. We preferred to emphasize the originality of the policy by choosing to use a newer word.

We had backed privatization even while still at university. It offered the exciting prospect of being able to roll back the state. People used to speak of a 'socialist ratchet', by which left-wing governments all over the world would introduce more state control and direction, but right-wing governments would be unable to reverse this when they took office because the measures would be too firmly embedded. Now with privatization we had the opportunity to reverse the ratchet, taking things out of the state sector in ways that would prove difficult for subsequent left-wing governments to reverse.

The Adam Smith Institute became fervent enthusiasts for privatization. We beat the drum for it on every occasion, writing articles and making speeches to popularize its appeal. We made the case for it systematic, analyzing the weakness of public sector supply and showing why these were endemic, rather than accidental, features of it. We explored the various different methods of privatization, showing why some were more appropriate than others for particular industries and services.

In our eyes privatization was not a series of policies but a system that fitted into a theoretical approach. Ultimately it brought to the administration and operation of services and industries the incentives, motivations and pressures that could improve them. The lack of these factors in public sector supply engendered the poor service quality and the serving of producer, rather than consumer, interests that characterized the public sector.

STRATEGY TWO

There was almost a recurring life cycle of Conservative governments. One would be elected and introduce a few reform initiatives. Invariably these took longer than anticipated and aroused protests that caused the government's resolve to wilt. Gradually the government would run out of steam, introducing more half-hearted and technical measures before the imminence of the next election put a final break on its radicalism.

During the early Thatcher government, commentators saw the

opposition that her policies had aroused for little gain in recompense, and they waited for the government to abandon its plans and veer back towards the centre or centre-left. However, there would be no U-turns for Mrs Thatcher. 'The Lady's not for turning,' she famously told the Conservative Party Conference, refusing to back down. If the policies had not yet yielded the required results, they must be continued until they did, or perhaps more radical ones might be introduced to bring home those results.

The government had been trying traditional methods of reforming the civil service and the public sector from within, bringing in outside people from business to show how they could be administered more efficiently. It did not solve the problem and, after the business types had left, the civil service simply reverted to type. I suggested light-heartedly that they came up with 'reforms' such as those which would involve using the paperclips twice, whereas what we needed to do was to take whole functions out of government and into the private sector, where competition would force them to cut costs and to address consumer concerns.

We recommended what we called *Strategy Two*. If the traditional approach was slowed by the opposition it aroused from vested interests, it might be time to try an alternative strategy that sought to appeal to other interest groups to counterbalance that opposition. The policies proposed in our *Strategy Two* paper were ones that used Public Choice analysis as a starting point for inventive ideas that would conjure up new interest groups to outweigh the old ones. Instead of trying to make state industries more responsive and efficient, they should be transferred to the private sector.

The privatization we were backing was not an economic strategy but a political one. It had to be done in a way that would stick, by calling into existence groups that would see they stood to gain. We needed ways of edging in competition so that its gains would be visible and immediate, and would not be at risk of future reversal.

Policies on education and health should win the support of significant groups such as parents and patients, to set against the opposition of the unions. Instead of trying to assuage trade union leaders, government should be reaching over their heads to bid for the support of their members.

Now! magazine was widely read by politicians and other journalists, and its editor, Tony Shrimsley, chose to give several pages to the Institute's *Strategy Two* approach, accompanied by full colour pictures. It presented the ASI paper's alternative approach as one that could succeed where the more traditional policies had failed to deliver. Other newspapers covered the ideas, which were seen as innovative and very radical, and we received high levels of interest from MPs and ministers.

The coverage of it prompted a remark from Arthur Seldon, a co-director of the IEA, at one of its receptions. 'You've been getting a lot of publicity for very little work,' he told us. It was not intended rancorously. He just thought that we should be publishing well-researched papers on economics, whereas we regarded our mission as different: we wanted to introduce new ideas into public policy discussion and to do so in ways that made them noticed.

It was perhaps in housing policy that the creation of new interest groups was most evident. Some 35 per cent of homes in Britain were state-owned council houses where people lived at subsidized rents. It seriously distorted the housing market and hindered mobility. Previous Conservative governments had sought to make council house rents more 'economic', (i.e. higher), but their tenants not surprisingly voted for uneconomic, lower rents. They preferred others to be taxed to finance their benefits, rather than be charged themselves for them.

While at university we had advocated transferring the ownership of such homes to their tenants, thereby ending the annual subsidy of their rents, but giving the tenants the possibility of becoming home-owners. We supported this because it made people less dependent on the state, in addition to it making more economic sense. We had even convinced Peter Walker, on a visit to Swinton College, that to dispose of council houses, even by giving some of them away if necessary, would get rid of the need to subsidize them permanently. It would be like a capital investment, buying lower operating costs in future.

The Conservatives in opposition had tentatively embraced the idea of selling council homes and now it introduced proposals in office to start this process. The existing tenants were offered discounts based on how long they had lived in their state homes paying rent. The discounts off the estimated fair market value started at 20 per cent and rose to 50 per cent (and later even higher). The point was to have the principle accepted. We could make the policy more robust once that had been achieved.

Opposition from local authorities, resentful of the loss of power this policy involved, was more than compensated by the support of those who opted to become home-owners. And as the Labour Party quickly realized, no government was going to be elected on a policy of taking away people's homes. The policy was thus irreversible and helped overturn the so-called socialist ratchet.

There was a feature about privatization which helped make it attractive to politicians. Government could tackle its spending needs to some extent by cutting but this is always difficult because of the political opposition it arouses from the affected groups. Government could raise taxes to bring in the revenues they sought but this, too, was unpopular with voters, most of whom thought taxes already too high. There was also the prospect of diminishing returns, as higher taxes might restrict economic activity and yield less revenue.

Government could use inflation, in effect printing money to finance its activities, and thereby reduce the amount that everyone else's money would buy. The Thatcher government had rejected this course – one followed recklessly by the previous Labour and Conservative governments – and had committed itself to making money honest again.

There was now a fourth way, however, namely using the cash yielded from privatization. Treasury accounting rules actually entered these proceeds as 'negative spending', whatever that is. It meant that government could use the money from sales to finance its activities without having to cut so severely, to raise taxes or to stimulate inflation. At the ASI, we treated politicians as an interest group and here was an advantage offered to them by privatization.

Of course privatization sales are one-off, in that they do not yield an annual revenue stream for government. Once the government has spent the proceeds of a sale, the money is gone, and they will have to sell more in the following year if they wish to keep spending that amount of money. This was fine by us. If it gave government an incentive to find yet more things to privatize each year, we regarded that as an advantage, not a drawback.

The former Prime Minister, Harold Macmillan, Lord Stockton, intervened to denounce privatization as 'selling the precious family silver to pay the butler's wages'. He was correct to note that privatization proceeds were capital and were being used to finance current spending. But he was absurdly wrong to compare Britain's state-owned industries to 'precious family silver'. Most of them were loss-making, dilapidated, inefficient and with a very low-quality output. It was more akin to unloading the family junk than to selling its silver. Indeed, Brian Walden, a one-time Labour MP, commented that the family silver had already been lost in a smash and grab raid by the trade unions.

We were regularly invited onto the media to make the case for privatization, and were happy to do so forcefully. It was a win-win situation in that the industries privatized would no longer need to be subsidized out of taxation. Instead they would be profitable private firms paying taxes rather than consuming them. They would become more responsive to consumers and competitive pressure would make them more efficient. Add to all this that the monies raised from privatization could help finance government activities. We were forceful advocates and spoke like true believers because that is what we were.

As the privatization programme unrolled, we found ourselves increasingly asked to explain it and expound it to foreign audiences as other governments began to show interest in an idea that had proved so successful. Privatization formed part of a worldwide return to markets and incentives, led intellectually by Nobel laureates Friedrich Hayek and Milton Friedman, but owing much to the practical success of Margaret Thatcher's governments.

We took the view that politicians in democratic societies will normally do things that are popular, or will pursue policies they think will bring them popularity when they are successful. They will not usually do things that fly in the face of popular opinion, but they will move onto ground that has been cleared for them. We took it to be part of our task to help clear that ground, to win acceptance in public for these ideas in order to make them acceptable options for politicians.

The Institute was a strident voice advocating the merits of

privatization, ever ready to argue and debate the case in public. We were helped considerably by the fact that privatization did actually deliver the goods. It brought the improvements that were claimed of it and its success in practice gave us powerful ammunition to make the case for more of it.

The Conservative government elected in 1979 did not go in with a shopping list of industries to be privatized. It would be more accurate to say that when they achieved a few early successes, this emboldened them to do more of it until the policy was roaring like an express train through the state industries and utilities. The Adam Smith Institute, by contrast, did have a shopping list; we wanted to privatize practically the entire state sector of the economy. On our list were the state utilities of telephones, gas, electricity and water. There were the state industries of coal, steel, car and truck manufacture, shipbuilding and aircraft manufacture. There were the state bus services, ferry services, the railways, plus the ports, the docks and the airports.

In publications and at seminars and conferences we made the case for privatizing all of these. In the process, we predicted, it would transform the British economy from being the sick man of Europe to becoming one of its economic leaders. Sometimes we put forward proposals as to how particular sectors might be privatized, but our biggest role was as advocates, urging that they *should* be privatized and spelling out some of the likely benefits which could be expected to follow. We chose to do this in public through the media, rather than privately to ministers, because we wanted to convince public opinion, and especially inform opinion about the superiority of markets, choices and incentives, and the merits of privatization. This required us to adopt a high profile and a somewhat combative one.

Privatization made a highly significant contribution to the

'reverse ratchet'. There was almost a regular progression in which the Labour opposition would oppose each item of privatization. After it went through they would pledge that a future Labour government would reverse it, taking the industry back into what they called 'public ownership' and we called state ownership. Then, when the policy succeeded and brought improvements in its wake, they would wait a year or two before dropping their pledge to reverse it. Privatization was transforming British industries and transforming the British economy, and it was not about to be undone.

PRIVATIZATION CONFERENCES

When foreign governments expressed an interest in privatization, or sent delegates on fact-finding tours in Britain to learn how it was done, the Foreign Office would always put us on the list of people to be visited, and we would make time to see them. The numbers of such delegations grew larger as the scale of privatization grew.

We still had just two directors and one or two interns, and began to think the time spent on this was not used efficiently. It did not benefit Britain at the time, though it soon began to do so as British firms found themselves hired to steer through privatization programmes in other countries. Indeed, it grew to be quite a significant industry for Britain. It was surreal to see so much money being made out of it while we still lived from hand to mouth, but we were the boffins, upstream leading-edge types, and it was the people from investment banks and accountancy firms that did the practical designs.

Rather than see these foreign delegations one by one as they came to visit, we decided to hold an international conference on privatization and try to address many of them together in one place. As speakers we engaged some of the people who had hands-on experience of privatization in Britain. We advertised the conference as widely as we could afford, which was not very much, in business papers such as *The Economist*, which had an international circulation.

The Economist at first refused to let us spell 'privatization' with a 'z' in our advertisement, because their house style (unlike *The Times*) had it with an 's.' We solved this by making the word part of a camera-ready artwork design that they could not change.

The Adam Smith Institute at that time had no real idea of how to organize conferences on this scale. It involved hundreds of delegates, many of them ministers, even prime ministers, and senior officials from all over the world, spread over two or three days. We had only done small, short ones for up to a few dozen people. Fortunately the interest of the subject matter won through. Our speakers had an enthralling story to tell, and the foreign delegates were there to learn it.

The conference was a success and made a significant contribution to our funds. People clamoured for us to do it again, so we added the Adam Smith Annual Conference on Privatization to our calendar, and held such conferences annually for a few years. In some years we booked the Queen Elizabeth Conference Centre, across from Westminster Abbey and Parliament Square. This was a very prestigious location, and had itself been partly privatized. One year we had a huge advertising display board fitted to the front of the building with our name and logo spread across it, unmissable to anyone passing by Victoria Street or heading towards Parliament. It did not bring additional delegates to the conference; they had all booked places weeks ago. What it did was to advertise the Institute itself and let people know we were there. It also brought us back into contact with a few old friends who happened to see it.

On a smaller scale we organized several conferences for local government councillors and officials, basically taking them through the process and best practices of contracting out local services to private companies. Although they were nothing like as grand as the Annual International Privatization Conferences, they played a useful role in spreading the ideas out to local authorities across the UK and again they aided our name recognition.

We had good feedback from local authorities on some of the problems they had encountered, and the steps they had taken or were taking to solve them. Some had pioneered some quite innovative privatization techniques and were happy to pass them on to other authorities. In particular we found that Kent County Council under Sir John Grugeon and Wandsworth Borough Council, where our St Andrews contemporary Chris Chope had been a councillor, had set the pace for reform, and we regularly included speakers from them on our programmes. This all added to our own expertise and increased the value of subsequent conferences.

From the conferences came publications. We would take some of the papers delivered and edit them into the chapters of a book. In the case of the Annual Privatization Conferences this produced some weighty tomes full of the practical experience of different types of privatization of different industries in different countries. They proved useful things to send out to people who wanted to learn about privatization without attending our conferences.

On the local government side we edited a series of smaller books dealing with the nuts and bolts of how to contract out services in ways that improved quality as well as saving money. Many of the conference papers had been delivered without a supporting written text, so had to be transcribed from recordings. Fortunately we had made contact with someone who could do audio typing and who had the rare ability to translate from spoken to written English. This was Sylvia Meek, and she turned what were sometimes rambling discourses into quite tightly drawn written chapters that could make up a book. Even though they still had to be edited, all of our speakers accepted the drafts, many amazed that their discursive remarks had been translated into so tight a text.

As with international privatization, there was a ready audience for practical books that gave lessons on how to contract out services, and what not to do. We stressed repeatedly that the whole bidding process had to be open and transparent, otherwise it might be open to accusations of corruption. We also stressed the importance of clearly set-out specifications detailing what standards the contractors would be required to achieve. Some local authorities who did this then found a profitable sideline in selling the contracts for other local authorities to use as models for their own. Southend were reported to have sold theirs at £100,000 a time.

Gradually privatization spread through Britain and the world, bringing improvements in the private sector operation of former state industries and services, improvements that would simply not have been possible had they remained with the state sector subject to political control. When the march of privatization eventually began to slow, it was not because it was running out of momentum. It was because it was running out of candidates.

7

THE OMEGA FILE

We noted that most governments tend to run out of steam and enthusiasm as their programme becomes bogged down and arouses opposition. Sometimes the initiative slips away from their reforming agenda and they drift towards the next election without the clear sense of direction that characterized their early months. Margaret Thatcher's government was far more robust than most when it came to pushing through reform, yet there were still many people, including even some of her own 'wet' ministers, urging her to slow everything down.

One of our responses to this was to highlight alternative policies, more radical ones, that might succeed where more conventional ones had not, and do so because they brought more consideration of how interest groups work in politics, and how support could be won and consolidated behind bold initiatives. This was the basis behind our *Strategy Two* set of ideas. The idea was to encourage people in government to re-radicalize their ideas while still in office. It was a theme we were to return to several times over the course of the years.

Our second response was a longer-range initiative. We noted

that governments that were sufficiently successful or sufficiently fortunate to win re-election would often then spend time devising a programme for their second term. As they prepared their agenda and priorities, precious months would slip away, leaving little time to set things in motion before things were bogged down again in delays and resolve was undermined by opposition.

We reasoned that if they had a fully prepared set of proposals and initiatives to draw upon as soon as they won office again, the time normally lost in preparation might be saved, and they could set about executing a programme of action. We did not know whether the government would do this for themselves, but we certainly intended to make helpful suggestions ourselves and to have an agenda ready to be embarked upon.

Thus was born the Omega Project. We wanted it to sound like the last word in policy innovation and the name also lent drama to it because it sounded like the title of a popular action thriller. When its findings became public, the name might enable it to command more attention. A law firm wrote to us claiming that one of their clients had copyrights on the name 'Omega', so we pasted together entries from the phone book and adverts for Omega watches and other Omega products and sent them copies. We never heard from them again. We had grown more confident since the days of *Inspector at the Door*.

For an organization as small as the Adam Smith Institute the project was on a stupendous scale. We calculated that we would need twenty working parties, involving a total of about 100 people to work for at least a couple of years on the project. The idea was that we would recruit a small group of between four and seven people to shadow each department of state. These would be people with some knowledge and expertise of the subject. They would study the responsibilities and activities of their department, and come up with a list of proposals to transform its output into something more compatible with choice and enterprise.

Each working party would have to meet several times. Their discussions would have to be written up and circulated. We certainly could not afford to pay any of those who took part, and could manage only modest expenses such as train fares. It was a daunting task, but we began to think of ways in which we might do it. The key to its success was to put the right person in charge.

Peter Young had just graduated from Aberdeen University, having spent a year's sabbatical as Chairman of the Federation of Conservative Students. He had worked closely with us during his year running FCS, and we had been impressed by his formidable organizational skills and ability to handle the details of a project. He had one thing in common with Eamonn and me: a boundless optimism that one could do anything if one went about it in the right way. Like us, he would set himself goals and then systematically go after them. He was twenty-one years old with curly hair, a boundless self-confidence and a reluctance to show deference to anyone in authority.

Peter was looking for something interesting to do, not necessarily something that paid well, but something that would express his own commitment to the same causes of freedom and enterprise that we ourselves espoused. He looked over our project outline and immediately began to suggest ways in which it might be developed and improved. He thought that it could, with difficulty and effort be done, and on a minimum budget at that.

We would have to pay him, of course, since he would need to move to London and support himself while running the project. We all thought it might take two years, with some working parties reporting in one year and others taking longer. The agreement was that we would seek sufficient funds to cover the expenses of the project and to pay him a sum that roughly amounted to what a sabbatical student based in London was paid. It was a very small sum, but he would be doing something he wanted to do and something he thought important.

It helped that university experience had taught him, like us, to live frugally. It also helped that he was able to find a council house tenant looking for someone to share the rent. This was against the rules, but there were so many council houses that huge numbers of people operated a kind of black market in sub-letting and passing on tenancy rights. And it helped even more when that particular tenant was convicted of armed robbery and sentenced to be detained during Her Majesty's pleasure, so Peter found himself house-sitting the council flat for a time.

The next step for us was to raise money to support the project. We approached three people. The first was Sir James Goldsmith. He listened carefully as we outlined the project, his eyes twinkling at the audacity and scale of it. Then he had his secretary hand us a cheque for £12,000 as we left.

Our next request was to Sir Clive Sinclair, the inventor. I had befriended him through Mensa, the high IQ society, where he served as chairman while I was its secretary. He wished that Britain could become more competitive and more open to those with talent and skills. He questioned us closely as we ran through the proposal, asking us about the actual process. He concluded that it would depend totally on the personnel involved, which was true, and asked to meet Peter Young personally before he committed himself. Peter went for an interview with Sir Clive and said he thought it had gone well. It must have done because Sir Clive sent us a cheque for £10,000 specifically to back the Omega Project.

The third person on our list of potential supporters was Sir

Malcolm McAlpine, a director of the McAlpine construction and civil engineering group. He often attended and took part in our activities, and we regarded him as a friend and supporter. We went to see him to ask for extra funds for the new project. He listened carefully, asking how we intended to run it. Finally he turned us down. He thought the idea was well conceived and very worthwhile, but said there was no way that we were capable of running it. We lacked the resources and the personnel, not to mention the infrastructure required to run so complex an operation.

He also cited the rather haphazard way we treated our subscribers, sending them some of our books but not others, not contacting them for months, then suddenly asking for more support. It was true. We were always more interested in promoting the ideas than we were in the mechanics of administration and managing our budget.

He was, of course, correct about the project. It was far too ambitious for us to undertake, given our very meagre resources. His opinion did give us pause for thought, but we did a few calculations on the back of envelopes and decided to go ahead anyway. We had just about enough backing from Sir James Goldsmith and Sir Clive Sinclair to set the project under way. Once it started, we might be able to raise more funds and even if we could not achieve all of it, the part of it we did manage to do would certainly be worthwhile.

We told Peter Young we were going ahead, so he joined the Adam Smith Institute as Director of the Omega Project. The next step was the choice of people to constitute the twenty working parties. Obviously we wanted people with qualifications as well as opinions on the department they were to cover. The Omega defence team, for example, included retired service officers and military commentators. The transport team included those with knowledge of bus, train, shipping, road and air transportation.

We drew on several sources. First were the academics who had published in the appropriate field. There were specialist writers who wrote on the various subjects. There were business people from the industries involved. Not least were the people making their way through a political career, people committed to the same causes as ourselves and with a more detailed knowledge of the political process. Finally there were retired civil servants who knew how departments worked and understood the processes of government.

All proved very willing to take part. In truth, they all regarded it as presenting an opportunity for them to express ideas which might influence events. Like us, they wanted to put forward ways in which things might be done better. Crucially, and based on our previous knowledge of how committees work, we made sure that every group contained at least one person who could write, someone who could draw together the points they all made and the ideas they put forward into a coherent whole that might be published.

The twenty working parties began to meet. This was no easy thing to arrange, since the Institute had no rooms suitable for holding them. Peter had to arrange for the groups to meet in rooms and offices outside. Some were borrowed from other institutes; some were offered by group members at their places of work or their home; sometimes the groups met in cafés or even hotel rooms. It was chaotic, but Peter's organizing ability managed to cope.

Each Omega group was sent at the start a brief prepared by Peter giving the remit of the department they were shadowing. The groups then met to discuss the perceived problems within each area, and to bring forward possible solutions. It was obvious at the outset that most of the groups were going to be very radical. The ideas they were proposing were very much along the theme of the Institute's *Strategy Two* approach, replacing the traditional ways in which departments had operated, and going instead for sweeping new ideas that could solve their problems, offering more freedom and more opportunities and incentives for enterprise in the process.

Peter had no secretarial help. He personally had to send notice of each meeting to its members, take notes at the meetings and then send the members summaries of what had been discussed and decided. He employed a young student part time (paid pocket money) as a bicycle courier to hand deliver the notices and summaries to the members of the Omega groups. The only other assistance he had was from Jennie Hunt, one of our two young employees, who helped him type up the final reports.

We could not offer to pay significant expenses to the participants, just the occasional train fare. One of the group covering the Scottish Office put in so absurd a claim to cover his expenses that we held subsequent meetings in Edinburgh, finding it cheaper to send the other members up there than to bring him down to London.

Given that there were a hundred people involved in the enterprise and meeting regularly, word began to trickle out that the ASI had a series of bold initiatives in the works that would set out a blueprint for changes that could transform the economy and society, and move Britain far away from the centre-left consensus which had been regarded as conventional wisdom.

A television producer asked if he could film part of one of the meetings, and other media people began asking us about the operation and whether they could trail any of its findings. Finally we agreed to co-operate with a BBC team who wanted to devote part of a programme to it. We gave interviews and allowed parts of it to be filmed. To our delight the producer had a board game made of the Omega Project, looking somewhat like a political version of monopoly, and used it in close-up to illustrate some of the Omega policies. He gave it to us afterwards as a souvenir, albeit without the tiny Lego characters he had borrowed from his son's toy box and had to return.

The groups were proceeding at very different paces, so we took the decision to publish each report when it was ready, rather than waiting for the whole lot to be completed as we had originally intended. It was as well we did, because some of the groups finished their work more than a full year after the others.

This had the effect of maximizing the coverage we achieved for the whole project. We were bringing out a series of twenty books, each covering the work of a different department of state or area of competence, and each with an agenda for the radical reform of that department. Each one would be released as a stand-alone report, though clearly part of a series that would run right through government.

As the first reports drew nearer to completion, the drafts were sent out to the members who had worked on them for any late alterations to be made. We wanted all the members of each Omega group to be in agreement on the final text of their report. While most people on the groups were happy to have their names listed in the preface, we only included those who assented. A few people, mostly for reasons connected with their employment, did not wish their names to appear and were therefore not included.

We gave some thought to the presentation of the finished reports. Finally we decided to have them all printed in A4 size, with a spine. They varied in size, depending on the scope of the department, but the average was between thirty and fifty pages. This made each of them look like an up-to-the-minute 'report' rather than a more substantial but libraryish and unexciting 'book'.

We took an idea from the supermarket shelves for our covers.

There were at the time generic products produced by the supermarkets without any big-name branding and selling much more cheaply than the branded equivalents alongside them on the shelves. Sainsbury's sold theirs in plain yellow packs with industrial stencil lettering in black spelling out such things 'Corn Flakes' or 'Washing Powder'.

We decided to produce the Omega reports as unbranded, 'generic' policy, also implying that they represented good value. Accordingly we produced each report in identical plain yellow covers, with the same industrial stencil letters spelling out the titles. The titles themselves were suitably bland, simply describing each as *The Omega Report on Energy* or *The Omega Report on Education*, as appropriate.

Before we started rolling out the reports we had one bad scare. Two reporters who had got wind of the project mistakenly thought the groups were secretly working on the 'real' Conservative agenda, and wanted to splash it in a Sunday newspaper as a secret Tory plot to destroy everything that was clean and decent in Britain. This would have caused difficulties in our relationship with the government, to put it mildly, and might have forced the Conservatives to reject in advance some of the ideas that the project was about to come out with.

Fortunately it was quite obvious that the Omega Project was an Adam Smith Institute undertaking, not a Conservative Party one. It would certainly have been better funded and more co-ordinated if it had been. We were able to use our friends in other sections of the media to pooh-pooh the scare story. Some of them were actually part of the Omega team and knew that it was far in advance of Conservative thinking.

The first of the studies to reach completion was the *Omega Report on Defence*. This might have been because the panel members included retired forces personnel who knew how to organize their time. Or it might have been that, having retired, they simply had more time to devote to it. They certainly knew what they wanted to say and expressed it in crisp, clear language.

A strong theme of their presentation was that Britain had not fully adjusted to the post-war world and the new scale and extent of its responsibilities. The UK kept a huge army on the Rhine to counter any Soviet offensive there, and had not taken on board the need to take swift action in far-flung places. The paper recommended that the Rhine army be halved and that a rapid deployment force should be created instead to react to our global responsibilities.

We launched the paper at a press conference in the House of Commons, in a committee room of the old Norman Shaw building that was formerly Scotland Yard. To my surprise it was packed with military journalists. After the paper had been introduced and the contributors had spoken briefly about different aspects of it, the panellists faced detailed questions from a highly knowledge-able group of experts.

As the questions and answers bobbed back and forth about the capabilities of various different types of hardware and systems, I realized that our authors knew their stuff. I certainly did not, because most of the jargon was over my head and I sometimes had no idea what they were talking about. It was obvious that they and the journalists mostly knew each other and got on well. They probably drank at the same clubs. The reporters clearly liked the paper and rather approved of its radical thinking.

This again showed the advantage of doing the reports separately. Each sector had its own national and trade press, who could cover it in much more detail than an omnibus report could have gained.

However much our authors might have known their stuff, we

certainly were somewhat lacking in knowledge of ours. We released the report when it was ready, without checking to see what else was going on that it might have clashed with. That something else turned out to be a big thing, for the *Omega Report on Defence* came out while the Prime Minister was visiting the British army on the Rhine. This caused some embarrassment.

Naturally the Prime Minister was confronted about the recommendations of the Omega report, and had to say that it was not her intention to halve the Rhine army. We simply had not been aware that our release clashed with the PM's visit. As it was, Mrs Thatcher's denial made all of the newspapers and the front page of some of them.

Helpfully, she did not dismiss the report out of hand. What she actually said was, 'The Adam Smith Institute is a very important institute, but it does not decide government policy.' It was good to have the Prime Minister describing us as 'very important', even with the added qualification. For some years afterwards when we spoke in the US, the people introducing us to meetings often quoted it. Many of them misquoted it by reporting the Prime Minister as saying that the ASI did not make government policy. We would then point out that what she had actually said was that we did not *decide* government policy.

The other Omega reports came out at steady intervals, and covered every single area of government policy. In all the ASI published nineteen of them. We had intended to make it twenty, but the one on Northern Ireland simply did not work, so we decided not to go ahead with it. It was below par, rooted in that place's past divisions rather than coming up with new and exciting changes for its future.

The nineteen papers in the series that we did publish amounted to a revolution in policy proposal. Taken together they presented a coherent account of an alternative Britain, one in which opportunities for choice and enterprise would replace the state's ownership and direction of its activities. From Education to Health, from Energy to Communications, from Transport to Industry, the Omega papers presented not just analysis, but a programme for action.

The *Omega Report on Local Government* even had a draft Act of Parliament appended. We grew so weary of being told by officials that its ideas 'simply could not be done' that we hired parliamentary draughtsmen to draw up a Bill showing how it *could* be done. The cleansing firm, Pritchards, agreed to fund it for us.

All of the reports received fairly good media coverage, with some featured on radio and television as well as in the newspapers. They were not released in any particular order, just as they came to be finished. As we released each one, that freed our time and energy to prepare the next one. They came out in a steady stream at roughly one report each month over a period of about a year and a half.

Several of those who were on the Omega working parties and contributed to its reports were elected to Parliament, and some even served as ministers to put into effect some of the ideas they had helped to develop. As the Omega reports were published, every Secretary of State save one invited the Omega authors to meet with them in their ministry and discuss aspects of the report. The one exception was the *Omega Report on Agriculture*, whose minister, John Gummer, refused to meet or to talk to any of the team. We had known each other since student days, and had not seen eye to eye even then.

One feature of the Omega reports was their practicality. We had politicians and civil servants involved in the process, so instead of just setting out aspirations or slogans, the proposals could have political and administrative practicality.

The final Omega paper we did was a collection of all nineteen reports published together in one volume. Even using double columns and a small typeface, it was still the size of a telephone directory. We called it *The Omega File*, and regarded it as the capstone to finish the project.

There was an epilogue: Malcolm McAlpine invited us to the elegant apartment that his company maintained above its offices, just off Russell Square in central London. He had noted the progress of the Omega Project and reminded us that he had declined to back the project because he did not think we were capable of doing it. Now he wanted to apologize and to congratulate us on proving him wrong. By way of further apology he later sent us a large cheque.

The Omega Project was a monumental undertaking that occupied our minds and efforts for the best part of two years. Many of the policy initiatives which first appeared in the Omega papers were subsequently implemented. A large-scale review of policy ranging right across government is something one might normally expect to be done within government, or at least within the workings of a major political party. This one was set in motion and directed by a handful of outsiders.

Early into her term in government, Margaret Thatcher had abolished the Central Policy Review Staff, sometimes dubbed the No. 10 think tank, or even colloquially as the Rothschild think tank, after its director, Lord Rothschild. A leaked paper on reforming the National Health Service had embarrassed the government and she had decided to wind it up. This left a small vacuum in forward policy thinking, one which the Adam Smith Institute and other think tanks were only too happy to fill.

Because we were outsiders, our ideas would not embarrass the government. It could listen to ones it liked, and ignore those it did not. That distance from government was useful to both sides. It left we think tanks free to be as radical as we liked, without government being tarred with the brush of some of our more outlandish ideas.

The Omega Project happened at a time when government was ready, indeed eager, to take on board ideas from outside. We ourselves were entirely happy to supply them. Omega might have been the last letter of the alphabet, but we soon realized it was not the final word in policy. Over the months and years that followed we came to realize that this was not how policy works. We had to say the same things, and new things, again and in different ways to different people. In policy a sound idea is just the starting point for debate rather than the jumping-off point for action.

8

NO TURNING BACK

The 1983 general election saw the overall Conservative majority increase to 144 seats, a big increase on the 1979 majority of forty-four. The myth among the chatterati was that this was achieved only because Margaret Thatcher's government had led the success-ful recovery and liberation of the Falkland Islands by British forces from Argentinean occupation. The reality was that the economy and the polls were turning her way even without the Falklands, and that the Labour Party had made an extraordinary lurch to the left. The prospect of a return to militant socialism was not one that appealed to the electorate.

The scale of the victory meant that Prime Minister Margaret Thatcher began her second term with many new faces on the benches behind her. Among those new faces were several friends we had known at the University of St Andrews, together with several of those who had worked on our Omega Project. In the newly elected Parliament they were 'new boys', and consequently lacking in authority and influence. The whips treated them as numbers to be marched through the lobbies to vote.

The group of those we had known at university or had worked

with were friends among themselves. They were nearly all of a similar age. More to the point, they all shared an outlook and philosophy similar to those espoused and expressed by the Adam Smith Institute. All believed that individuals generally make better choices about their lives than the state can ever manage, and that this was true of people's personal lives as well as their economic affairs.

They all shared something else, too, which was the feeling that the government was not making sufficient progress towards these goals. Too many of the Cabinet seemed to be still aligned to the centre-left policies which their party had adopted for most of their political lives. They drew on the tradition of Harold Macmillan and Edward Heath and the post-war consensus. By contrast the new breed of younger members wanted something different. They felt that those policies had contributed to Britain's decline, whereas now it was time to reverse it.

The group included Michael Forsyth, Peter Lilley, Michael Portillo, Chris Chope, Michael Fallon and Robert Jones and perhaps another ten like-minded persons. They began meeting regularly to discuss what they saw as the 'drift' of government and the danger that very little would be achieved before the next election loomed. They wanted to do something about it.

I had known about this peripherally from the occasional social meeting, but was not involved personally. This was a group of Conservative Members of Parliament, and was very much more 'party' and political than we had chosen to be. Our aim was to influence ideas and events, rather than to become involved in the day-to-day business of politics.

The first I knew of what had been happening was when I was invited to dinner in the House of Commons by Michael Forsyth. We had been closely involved with Michael not just at university but subsequently in the campaign to contract out local government services, and later in promoting privatization in other areas.

Michael produced a huge pile of papers, several inches thick, and placed them on the table. He told me the group had decided to publish their ideas on the way Britain should proceed, and had been working on a paper that would express them. They hoped this would be the focus for fresh thinking about the direction of government. He looked at the pile in some despair and added that several of the members had set out their thoughts on paper, and that they had been trying to pull it all together into some coherent document. After three months of struggling to make some sense and unity of it, they had decided to try a different tack.

Michael then asked me if I would be prepared to produce a draft, putting together their ideas into a single paper they could then work on, modify, add to and then publish under their joint names. I thought about it briefly, then said I would, if they met two conditions. The first was that I wanted to be paid £1,000 for my work. This was quite a sum at the time and the money was important because I could have used the time to earn money elsewhere, but my real reason was that I wanted them to value what I did.

My second condition was that I would not have to pick up the pile of papers he had deposited on the table. My reasoning was straightforward. It is a very difficult task to edit together the writings of several authors, all with their different styles and emphases. They had been trying for months without success.

I did not need to. I had known these people, either as friends or as colleagues or as both. I knew the philosophical position they took and the types of policy they would like to see used to transform Britain. They were ideas we all had in common. It would be far easier for me to write them up *de novo*, and then have them edit it and agree upon a final wording afterwards.

We talked further and Michael told me their view that there were four key policy areas they wished to be covered. First came education, at both school and university level. Then there was health, and the problem of a producer-directed system and falling standards. Next came employment, and of market solutions to the persistent high unemployment that had been a product of Britain's declining competitiveness. Finally there was housing, with subsidized state sector council houses, rent controls and planning restrictions still blighting the emergence of a genuine market that could produce the housing people wanted. It was quite a challenge.

What made it easier was that all of these areas had been addressed in the Omega Project, on which several of those who were now Members of Parliament had worked. It became a question of explaining the ideas in a concise form. It seemed that a brief introduction might analyze the problems in each area, then short chapters could follow explaining the proposed policies that could address those problems.

The actual process of preparing the draft was aided by a friend who gave me the use of his house while he was away at work each day. For several days I set off with a portable computer (then about the size of a suitcase) and crossed London to where he lived. I worked during the day in a totally empty house, leaving only when he returned home after work. The first draft was ready within days.

The key to education was the virtual voucher. Parents had to be empowered in some way so that their choices would influence the quality of their child's education. Vouchers had the political weakness that they were new and strange, and parents could easily be scared by left-wing campaigners into supposing that they would have to pay for a state education that might be beyond their means. Every attempt to introduce vouchers over a period of more than two decades had been thwarted by the opposition of teachers' unions and left-wing activists.

The Omega solution was to make the vouchers virtual, and not to use the V-word at all. A way of hiding the vouchers had first been formulated in discussions at our Westminster flat, and incorporated into the *Omega Report on Education*. If parents were free to choose schools, and if the state funding for their child went to the school they had chosen, this was, in effect, a voucher system without the dreaded pieces of paper. This policy was what the group of MPs wanted to urge the government to adopt, so it became a question of putting their wishes into a form that made it look attractive and compelling. The interest and support of parents could outweigh the self-interest of the teaching unions.

A similar approach could transform health policy. If patients were allowed to choose between providers, with the money following their choices, consumer pressure would be introduced into the health services in a way that would lead to improvements in patient care. It was almost certain that this would also introduce efficiencies and savings, enabling the service to deliver more and better health care for any given level of funding.

In the case of housing it came down to extending the rights and abilities of council house tenants to buy their own homes. Very many council homes were flats rather than individual houses, so it needed forms of ownership introduced to cope with this fact. Legislation was needed to facilitate the ability of block associations to own the freehold, assigning part of it to the individual flats, thus enabling them to be purchased. The discounts could be extended, giving many more tenants the rights and the ability to buy their own homes.

The solution on employment was a reaction against past efforts at job creation by government, either by subsidizing existing employers, both state and private, or by trying to 'pick winners' and help fund new industries. The alternative approach would concentrate on creating the conditions under which free enterprise could create wealth and jobs spontaneously. We had described this as a policy of 'pull' rather than 'push', because much of it required government to get out of the way.

It needed both taxes and regulations to be lowered, especially for small businesses, so that it would become worthwhile for entrepreneurs to take the risk of setting up new businesses, and in doing so to create the new jobs that would help soak up the unemployment. They would, in the process, also create wealth that could be taxed and would contribute to the national exchequer, instead of depleting it by subsidies and supports.

Small businesses have a crucial part to play, in that they generate most of the new jobs, and represent the future. Those companies that become the giants of business very often started life as small businesses. In making life easier for the start-up enterprises, we would be creating the small employers of today as well as the big employers of the future.

Michael circulated the draft to the group of MPs, and took in their comments and suggestions. I guessed they had been mostly favourable because very few changes were made. Fortunately none of them tried to edit the prose and alter its natural flow. My involvement with it was now over, and nowhere was there any mention of, or connection to, myself or the Adam Smith Institute. They paid me my £1,000 and we were all happy.

Somehow they persuaded Conservative Central Office to sanction this report's publication under the imprint of the Conservative

Political Centre. It appeared in 1985 under the title *No Turning Back*, which gave its name to the group.

Its publication was well received by the media and it received extensive press coverage, including the front page of at least one national daily. The political correspondents spotted the significance of it. Here were more than a dozen, mostly of the new intake of MPs, making a plea for a more rapid extension of free-market ideas, and into areas hitherto untouched.

In effect they were declaring their independence and marking themselves off from the more traditionally minded members of the party. They were saying that Thatcherism ran much deeper than the Prime Minister and her circle, and calling upon them to draw on those backbench reserves of support.

Their purpose in going ahead with the publication was to oppose any reversion to traditional 'managerial' policies, and instead keep the government committed to a radical, free-market agenda. An additional consequence, which might not have featured in their planning, was that it drew attention to them. They emerged from obscurity to be the group that people were talking about, and it made the party managers and the whips office take notice of them. This did no harm at all to their subsequent political careers.

They began holding regular dinners at the IEA to discuss the state of the government and to co-ordinate actions to keep it on a radical course. It was not very long before Michael invited me to another dinner in the House of Commons. I guessed correctly what was coming. They wanted to do it again, but with a narrower focus. This time they wanted to concentrate on the one area of education, and set out in detail the mechanisms that would take control of it from the departmental civil servants and teaching unions, and hand it to the parents.

This was a real battleground because the left strongly opposed the idea. They saw schooling as a way of indoctrinating children with their own left-wing attitudes and ideas, and of implementing fashionable ideas about 'unstructured' (and unmeasurable) education. They knew that if parents had any choice in the matter, nearly all of them would choose schools which practised a more traditional and disciplined approach, and which taught the children to read and write, to value learning, to pass exams and which would do their best to inculcate good manners in them.

We discussed the form the paper might take, concentrating mostly on the schools, but with some attention given to the universities. It was to be an expansion of the education ideas set out in *No Turning Back*, which were themselves very much in line with the principles set out in the *Omega Report on Education*.

The aim was to reverse the top-down direction of education and replace it by a bottom-up model in which the priorities and choices of parents would determine the standards and distribute the resources. It was an internal market, in that state funding would continue, but the production of education would be taken out of the state's hands. The state would simply be buying education, on behalf of the parents, from many different providers, just as a customer might do in a real market. It was not the privatization of education, because the state would still guarantee a free school place for every child.

A choice between worthless schools is no choice at all, so there had to be mechanisms by which poor schools would face incentives to improve and by which new schools could be opened. It was envisaged that concerned parents and teachers might join forces with local business people to found new schools in areas where there was a shortage of places at good schools.

The funding was to be based on the number of children who enrolled at the school, rather than on the allocation of funds by the local education authorities. The funding for a child of each age group would, in effect, follow the child. If parents withdrew a child from a school they deemed unsatisfactory, that school would lose the child's annual allocation. Meanwhile the school which the parents had chosen instead would now receive that allocation.

To be effective, it would have to be easy for parents to move their children between schools and even to start new ones. The impediments of local planning controls and the lengthy process for planning permission could be overcome by the introduction of a 'fast track' status for school applications. It was important that local education authorities should have no say in this process, since it was envisaged that they would jealously guard their existing powers and attempt to thwart the establishment of new schools out of their control.

I wrote the draft of the paper in very much the same way as I had for their first publication, going away with my computer each day for a few days until it was done. Once again the MPs liked the draft, and very few changes were made to it. I was paid £1,000, as I had been for the previous one. It was published, like the first, by the Conservative Political Centre in a similar format and design. The group chose the title *Save Our Schools.*

It did not have quite the media impact of the first one, perhaps because it was less surprising, but it did receive extensive coverage, including feature articles and editorials in newspapers. On the table now was a viable alternative to the then-current system of running and funding schools, and it was radically different.

Furthermore, this was not the voucher system which people had several times attempted to stage local trials of – without success. This was a new policy that was designed to achieve the same as vouchers sought to achieve, but it was crafted to appeal more to parents.

After two successful publications setting out policy initiatives the *No Turning Back* Group was now firmly established on the political landscape. They went on to publish more, but the increasing workload of the Adam Smith Institute now took so much of my time and energy that I could no longer be involved with the group's output. Their third publication, *Health – A Suitable Case for Treatment*, made the case for choices by patients to introduce market-based reforms into the monolithic health service.

It had been a useful association, however, and the group all became good friends and supporters of the Institute, and a regular feature at our events. It helped our general mission that we were perceived to have a significant number of young MPs involved with us. Most of the group went on to take up posts as junior ministers or ministers of state, and four of them – Michael Forsyth, Peter Lilley, Michael Portillo, John Redwood – later joined the Cabinet.

Some of the ideas set out in their publications subsequently made their way into legislation, although the legislative proposals were never as clear and coherent as the policy proposals had been. This is usually what happens as a result of the political process and the way in which laws are made. Influential as they were on legislation, though, the group's publications achieved something no less important. They set forth ideas that derived from a clear and coherent philosophy, one strikingly different from that which had formed the backdrop of recent decades of parliamentary activity.

There was one further message implicit in the exercise. It was that people were looking beyond the current privatization programme then picking up speed through the state-owned businesses. There were industries still to be privatized, and then there were the state utilities including energy generation and supply, communications and transport. Beyond them and still over the horizon lay the state services of education, health and welfare. Now people were beginning to point in that direction.

9

SCOTLAND AND OTHER COUNTRIES

The Adam Smith Institute has always had a complicated relation-ship with Scotland. On the plus side we were popularizing the name and ideas of one of Scotland's greatest sons, the father of modern economics. All three of the ASI's founders had been partly educated in Scotland, had lived there for a time and all had degrees from Scottish universities. We were also propagating ideas some of which had been incubated during our spell at the University of St Andrews.

The Scottish media and establishment were rather less keen on the fact that we were putting forward ideas which were not in accord with the current outlook of Scotland. The nation returned a majority of Labour MPs to Parliament and most of its major conurbations were under the control of Labour local governments. There was, furthermore, a 'Red Clydeside' tradition of policies well to the left of the Labour Party. Free-market libertarian ideas were simply out of accord with Scottish support for state direction, ownership and control. They liked centralized planning; we espoused the spontaneous order of the market.

During the years that Conservative governments were returned in Westminster, the Scots were very conscious of the fact that they had not voted for those governments. In fact the number of Tory MPs from Scotland steadily declined. Yet here were people who had gone from Scotland to London, via the US, and had set up a think tank to influence the future of the UK and, if we could, the thinking of a generation.

Moreover, the ASI's colours in its logo and on its heading were light blue, dark blue and white, chosen because they were the colours of the University of St Andrews. On the wall of the ASI office was hung – and still hangs – a huge saltire, the diagonal white cross on blue that is the national flag of Scotland. It had been made for me by one of my Hillsdale students.

When the ASI built a mezzanine floor to provide a meeting room within its office, it was christened the 'St Andrews Room', and featured a huge curved mural of St Andrews as it was in 1693, reproduced from the engraving by Captain John Slezer in *Theatrum Scotiae* (and conveniently masking some unsightly pipework). In other words there was a strong Scottish flavour to the Institute, even though its ideas were not in accord with current Scottish thinking.

The result was that we featured regularly in the Scottish media. They were eager to cover our reports and our initiatives. They frequently interviewed us on Scottish radio and TV, and invited us to contribute feature articles. There was a half-hour TV programme about the Institute and its St Andrews origins, with shots and interviews of us intercut with those of the university and its students. 'They were singing the praises of the free market,' said the presenter, with the picture showing us, then moving to a choir in the university chapel. I commented to Eamonn, 'Never have the praises of free markets been sung so sweetly.'

Since Douglas Mason was one of our writers and still lived in Scotland at Glenrothes in Fife, we had a sort of Scottish presence. He was, incidentally, one of the millions who had bought his own council house. Douglas was always ready to be interviewed in Scotland at short notice about some of our ideas. He had been heavily involved with the *Omega Report on Local Government*, and was himself a local councillor who understood the details of local government responsibilities.

Douglas began to write a series of policy papers for us exclusively covering Scottish matters. His *Road to the Isles* recommended the full privatization and end of monopoly and subsidy of ferry services between the Scottish mainland and islands. *Wood for the Trees* urged the privatization of the Forestry Commission, which had a deplorable record in Scotland, having covered large parts of the land in regimented rows of uneconomic identikit conifers.

Douglas broke new ground with his *Livingston plc, I Presume*, suggesting that the Scottish new towns, of which there were five, should be modelled on the Spanish Mondragon community as business entities owned by their residents. All of these and others were extensively covered in the Scottish media, featuring interviews with Douglas and articles by him.

Some years before Hong Kong was finally handed over to Chinese rule, Douglas wrote a somewhat tongue-in-cheek paper, *A Home for Enterprise*, suggesting that one of the Scottish islands should be set aside as a home for anyone from Hong Kong who wished to live there. He made the point that if they were allowed to enjoy similar tax and regulatory rules as Hong Kong had enjoyed, there could be a massive and unprecedented boost to the Scottish economy.

Douglas made it clear to us that the real motive behind his piece was to strengthen the UK's negotiating position with the

Chinese government. The government might well concede more by way of democracy and civil liberties, he told us, if it thought the Hong Kong people had the option of going elsewhere. Douglas was also showing how burdensome British taxes and regulations were compared with those of Hong Kong, and how vibrant Hong Kong was by comparison.

His nuanced arguments cut no ice with the Scottish papers, which were mostly hostile to non-socialist thinking. They were outraged at the possibility of up to 3 million Chinese coming to live offshore and becoming part of the Scottish population. One popular cartoonist suggested that it was a deep plot by Margaret Thatcher to add 3 million Chinese Tory voters to the Scottish electorate!

The Scottish media establishment kept urging the ASI to set up a branch in Scotland and do the same kind of work at a Scottish level that we had been doing at a UK level from London. We considered it very carefully and looked over budgeted plans to see if it might be viable. We decided it was not. Basically we still had almost no money coming in, and since neither Eamonn nor I wanted to abandon the Westminster scene, that meant we would have to recruit Scottish staff to run a branch in Edinburgh or Glasgow. That raised problems of trying to control the operation at a distance.

It is possible that if our hearts had been in it, we might have been able to put a group of Scottish worthies together to raise the funds for it, and then hire some bright youngster in Glasgow or Edinburgh to propagate some of the ideas we were advocating at a national level, and to construct Scottish equivalents of some of the policy initiatives we were putting out.

But we were always lukewarm about setting up any kind of Scottish branch. We felt it unlikely that the Scots would be as receptive to our ideas as others had been, and that a great deal of effort on our part would have achieved very little. We also took the view that what would work in Scotland was the same agenda of free enterprise, markets, choice and incentives that we advocated generally. It was not that Scotland needed something different and distinctive, simply that the Scots showed less enthusiasm for turning to the private sector to create wealth, opportunities and employment.

We thought Scotland definitely needed these ideas, and eventually we went through the motions of setting up a limited Scottish presence. We had separate publications made, tailored to a Scots audience, and created a Scottish leaflet stressing our Scottish origins and connections. We even held a series of conferences and seminars in Scotland, though they were by no means as well attended as our London ones. We concluded that there were simply not enough like-minded people there from which to assemble a critical mass that might help turn around policy in Scotland.

Lord Goold, a Scottish supporter and director of the building firm MacTaggart & Mickel, obligingly allocated us an office roughly the size of a broom cupboard in one of the firm's Glasgow offices just off Blytheswood Square, and we installed a separate telephone and answering machine. This gave us an address and telephone number in Scotland, though the office was never manned. We simply accessed the answering machine remotely and responded to any callers who needed a reply.

Even this tenuous experiment came to an abrupt end when the building had to be completely redeveloped when 'sick building syndrome' was suspected. With the closure of the building went the little office that we had never visited even once.

Fortunately, the transport connections between London and Scotland improved to such an extent that we were able to visit regularly and be visited without needing a base in Scotland. We always had a bias toward recruiting interns and gap-year students from Scotland anyway, so our office in London was never devoid of Scottish accents. Added to that the *Sunday Post*, Scotland's largest circulation paper and one of the very few that took a right-of-centre position, decided it liked us, and regularly asked us to pen articles on topical issues. This kept our ideas and our presence before the Scottish public.

When Michael Forsyth was appointed Chairman of the Scottish Conservative Party, it reinforced our connection with Scotland since he was known to be associated with the Institute and had authored some of its reports. He chose as his chief of staff Russell Walters, who had been our second gap-year employee, further strengthening the connection. But the idea of establishing any kind of Scottish office or base there gradually faded from our priorities as we became busier.

THE WASHINGTON OFFICE

Several of our US friends asked us to consider setting up an office or a branch in Washington DC in order to spread our ideas there. This interested us because both Eamonn and I regularly visited Washington as we accepted speaker invitations in the US. We also reckoned that there was much more support for free-market and free-choice ideas in the US than we had ever found in Scotland. Indeed, what held us back was the recognition that there were already several successful US think tanks that promoted the same sorts of ideas that we did, and were large and well funded.

Eventually, after the Omega Project was completed, we decided to dip a toe in the water by setting up a small US operation and to see if we could make any impact. We suggested to Peter Young that he might want to lead this, and he readily assented. He moved over to Washington and took a lease on a house on Capitol Hill. It was on the very edge of what was considered 'safe' territory, and was only a couple of blocks west of an area where crime and drugs were commonplace. It therefore had an advantage of not being too expensive.

What we had done in London, Peter did in Washington: using the house both as a place to live and as an office. Gradually it acquired basic furniture and equipment, and Peter used it as a base from which to do the rounds of the US think tanks and to take part in their seminars. He testified before Congressional Committees and was interviewed in US publications, but his more basic task was to raise sufficient funds to cover the costs of the operation.

Nevertheless the operation was always held back by lack of money. There was never enough to undertake ambitious projects. It produced a few publications, but faced the problem that there was such a storm of these continually coming out in Washington so it was very hard for new ones to capture sufficient attention. There was also a certain reserve arising from the fact that we were perceived as 'foreign'. We were British, and although our name and our work in Britain were quite widely known about in US policy circles, we were looked upon as a curiosity in Washington. We spoke with British accents and, although these were generally admired in the US, they did mark us as different and raised questions about whether we were properly qualified to talk about US policy.

One big success was the relationship we build up with the American Legislative Exchange Council (ALEC), which represented over 2,000 state legislators and several members of Congress. They organized speaking tours for me to visit a series of US state legislatures and address the state assemblies. The subject they were interested in was the privatization of state services, drawing on the experience in the UK of bringing in private contractors.

The tour culminated in their annual gathering in Florida, with over a thousand representatives at an open-air dinner in Orlando with me as the speaker. My speech was delayed by a rather dramatic electric storm that swept through the place illuminating the night with great jagged flashes of lightning. I think any speech would have gone down well amid the relief that followed when it was over.

We had close relations with another US group: the National Center for Policy Analysis (NCPA), based in Dallas. It was headed by Dr John Goodman, a health expert we had invited to address our Windsor Castle conferences. Now we had a US presence and reasons to visit regularly, the link between the ASI and the NCPA grew stronger. Although NCPA was a think tank which covered the range of policy issues, they held a commanding position at the forefront of health reform, and we published many of John's papers on the subject in the UK and featured him regularly at our conferences.

Similarly he published material by us in the US, and invited Eamonn and me to speak at NCPA conferences. He published a book by me on privatization and ensured it received widespread attention. It introduced the idea to many American readers for the first time, and resulted in yet more invitations to speak and to write.

Both Peter and I made several presentations before the 'Wednesday Meetings' which Grover Norquist organized to link think tanks on the right and centre right, and to help them co-ordinate their activities. They were useful because they were always attended by White House aides and assistants to the President, in addition to the think tanks and campaigning groups, and they have since grown into a national institution. I first met Grover through mutual friends in Washington years earlier when he was fresh out of college. Even then he was a formidable organizer and political operator.

There were other successes achieved by the US operation during its few years, but lack of funding took its toll. Eventually Peter grew tired of living on a shoestring and wanted to return to the UK to start a new business that would draw on his experience on influencing legislators in the UK and the US. We decided to close down the US operation and did not renew the lease on the house on Capitol Hill.

In the days before Skype, the internet and e-mail it was difficult to co-ordinate between the UK and the US, and much harder to know what was happening and whether the results were worth the effort put in.

CANADA

The Adam Smith Institute had good relationships with a number of think tanks and similar organizations in other parts of the world. We would often meet their personnel at meetings of the Mont Pelerin Society and, in addition to exchanging ideas, we would often arrange to co-operate on joint activities.

In Canada we were on good terms with the Fraser Institute, based in Vancouver, and made a few exchange visits. The Canadian group we were most involved with, however, was the National Citizens' Coalition (NCC). This was a group representing Canadian citizens concerned about high taxes, government waste and similar issues. It was a campaigning organization, and a very successful one. It was backed by John Dobson, a successful businessman and philanthropist with a penchant for free-market ideas and leaner government. He subsequently supported some of the ASI's work as well.

Based in Toronto, but with branches across Canada, the NCC was headed by David Somerville, a committed and highly effective organizer. We met at a meeting of the Philadelphia Society, a US society for business people and academics who supported the free-market economy. I was on the programme and David invited me to travel up to Canada to deliver a similar talk to his group.

It was the start of a long-term association and friendship. I made many trips all over Canada, speaking to their groups and doing TV interviews. There were side pleasures to be enjoyed along the way because David was a keen fly fisherman, and several times took me fishing for trout and salmon when the opportunity presented itself just before or immediately following one of these speaking trips.

The NCC published several pieces by me, including one on privatization geared to the Canadian experience. David would regularly have me meet Canadian politicians to outline possible strategies to limit the seemingly inexorable growth of government.

On one of the trips to Canada's western provinces, I found myself in a giant marquee addressing a dinner of 1,200 people. As I'd arrived in Alberta I had turned on the TV in my hotel bedroom to discover that I was the first item on the evening news or, more correctly, that the demonstration against my visit and talk was the lead item. I rather liked the placard that read, 'Pirie, keep your privates to yourself'. Those attending the dinner outnumbered the demonstrators by a hundred to one, however.

FRANCE

Having seen what was going on across the Channel, several French think tanks contacted us. They wanted to get on top of it and maybe have a taste of it themselves. A succession of French institutes came to visit us in London, or invited me over to speak in Paris.

The problem in France was that the think tanks were usually tied to the career of a particular politician. If the star of that person faded, then the think tank saw its funding and influence diminish accordingly. At least a dozen such groups came and went during the late 1970s and early 1980s. Our one constant link with France was Henri Lepage, a leading member of the Mont Pelerin Society, author of the influential *Demain le Capitalism* and an adviser to Alain Madelin.

Some of our books were translated into French by Francois Guillaumat, a French libertarian and free marketeer, and were published there, but there was a cultural problem as well as an organizational one. The relationship between Britain and France made it unlikely that the French would ever want to copy something that had been pioneered in the UK. They would prefer something uniquely French, something that touched their cultural concerns as well as their economic and political problems.

There was an intellectual hurdle, too. The French seem to prefer great sweeping systems of thought, perhaps in the tradition of Descartes. The approach being used in the UK, of experimentation and repeating the things that worked in practice, did not sit easily with the French tradition. I was asked about these differences of style on several occasions. Once, when I started to explain that I subscribed to what I called 'the English national philosophy of empiricism', it drew a ripple of laughter, and my hosts explained that they use 'empiricism' to mean the absence of a philosophy.

I found that if I spoke in English, French audiences would listen politely (though rarely enthusiastically), often preferring to follow my English rather than the simultaneous translation. If I spoke French, they would listen animatedly and join in lively discussions afterwards. Since my French vocabulary was not up to speeches about modern economics, I used to write them in English, have

Francois translate them, then deliver them in French after I had practised a few times.

For all the visits and exchanges of ideas, I found the French remained more comfortable with a 'command and control' approach to political economy. What to us was the complex inter-action of different participants and the emergence from these of a spontaneous order seemed to the French people I met to look more like the working of chance, and lacking the rationality of a directed order.

The thing that puzzled me about France was that it did so many things wrong, yet still managed to enjoy a decent standard of living and an economy that could more or less hold its own internation-ally. Given that they decided things on a political basis, rather than let the market allocate resources where they were needed, it seemed remarkable that they performed as well as they did.

SCANDINAVIA

The other countries that occupied some of our attention were Denmark, Norway and Sweden. Perhaps my own Scandinavian roots helped direct my interest, but the ASI's involvement began when three young Danes attended one of the summer ISOS sessions at Cambridge. They were free-market libertarians, and decided to start an association for like-minded people in Denmark. We gave them very modest help with free publications and free places at our conferences, and began to make regular visits to address them.

In the course of such meetings we encountered people from Norway and Sweden as well, and started to interact with groups in those countries. A steady stream of young Scandinavians, mostly Danes, began to apply for our gap-year positions and internships, and our office often had a Scandinavian as well as a Scottish air to it.

They began to introduce us to up-and-coming legislators – and later ministers – when we went to speak to their groups, so it provided an avenue for us to put across policy ideas. Usually the youngsters managed to get their newspapers to cover the speeches we gave at their conferences as well.

We probably helped to put across free-market ideas to more young Scandinavians than would otherwise have encountered them, but the more we learned about their governments, the more we changed our opinion. We had tended to assume, as conventional wisdom had it, that the Scandinavians epitomized the 'social' model of the economy, with high taxes and government regulation and direction.

We found that the reality was more complex, with high taxes to support transfer payments and state services, but very much lighter regulation and direction than we had supposed. Indeed, the Scandinavian states came high on the international freedom list of countries amenable to free enterprise. It would have been more accurate to call them relatively free-market states in which government intervention in the economy took the form of taxation rather than regulation and control. As such, it is less surprising that we found ready ears in their legislatures for free-market ideas and initiatives.

The final irony was that we had started by speaking in Sweden in support of the initiatives being taken in Britain to loosen up state control and allow more free choices by individuals. Over time, however, we found ourselves advocating in Britain the reforms that the Swedes had taken in both education and pensions. They had undertaken bold initiatives to break up monolithic state provision into services that were largely decided by the personal choices made by their citizens.

10

THE FORTUNE ACCOUNT

The Adam Smith Institute first visited the subject of pensions in its *Omega Report on Social Security*. Pensions in the UK had long been a hot political issue, and there were always demands for the level of the state old age pension to be raised. Since there were approximately twice as many people over sixty as there were people under thirty, and since they were twice as likely to vote, the elderly had roughly four times the political clout of the young.

This mattered under a pay-as-you-go pension system and Britain's state retirement pensions follow this model. Under this system there is no fund invested to pay the future needs of pensioners. Instead money taken from today's workers in taxation is distributed to today's pensioners. It is a straight transfer system. Politicians promise benefits today, but make future generations pay for them tomorrow.

To some extent this sets the interests of the young against those of the old. The one group has to pay more taxes so the other can have higher incomes. This balancing act can be sustained over long periods, but faces problems from changing demographics. If people live longer, as they now tend to, more of them have to be supported, and for a longer period.

The ASI authors calculated that at the time of the Beveridge Report one retiree was supported by five workers. The balance had shifted since then, and the ratio was now one to three, heading towards one to two. They told us that when Beveridge wrote the report, a typical man worked for the same firm from the age of sixteen to the age of sixty-five, then lived an average of two more years in retirement. Now they might expect to live perhaps twenty years in retirement instead of two. As a result the system was creaking.

The Institute looked at the solutions tried in other countries, especially at the pensions policies pursued in Singapore and Chile. Neither of these had a pay-as-you-go system, and both had opted for funded systems. In pay-as-you-go systems people pay taxes and receive a state pension when they retire, but under a funded system people save money in personal pension accounts instead, and have their own pension paid from that fund on retirement. It gives them a degree of independence from government.

There is a crucial difference: the personal pension fund allows for choices to be made and grows with the growth of the economy. It is thus much less affected by changing demographics and greater longevity. It has the incidental advantage that these funds build up into huge sums available for investment capital.

The Adam Smith Institute published reports comparing the Chilean pension system with that of Singapore (which includes other needs as well as retirement pensions), and picking out the best features of each that might be incorporated into a funded UK system. We called this *Singapore versus Chile*. The biggest problem was the transition. All of the advantages might lie with a funded system, but how could the UK pay-as-you-go system be transformed into one?

We published *The Fortune Account*, suggesting the gradual replacement of state pensions by private ones. New workers would be required to contribute to private pension plans, and older workers would be given the choice to do so up to a cut-off point, with incentives to make their choices easier. Approved providers would manage these pensions, with periodic opportunities for pension-holders to switch between providers.

A key point was that the government would honour the promises it had made to current workers, and in no way undermine the state pensions it had promised. The Fortune Accounts would offer a much better deal, however, since they would be invested in products that broadly reflected the long-term growth of the economy. They would be able to provide pensions very much better than any the state could hope to offer.

The Fortune Account attracted some heavyweight public support from Members of Parliament and financial journalists. They liked the idea that there was a valid alternative to the state's pay-as-you-go system with the burdens it placed on future shoulders and one which future governments might not be able to finance.

Our proposal involved a degree of compulsion in order to surmount the Treasury objections that would have arisen otherwise. The Treasury would have taken a dim view of voluntary private pensions that left the state picking up the tab at the end for those who had preferred to be profligate. We pointed out that the current system involved compulsion, too, in that payment of taxes and National Insurance is by no means voluntary under the state-financed system.

While we were wondering how best to put this proposal firmly in the public domain among the other options available for consideration, we heard news that José Piñera, the former minister who had helped craft and implement the Chilean pensions reform, was coming on a visit to Britain. We hastily put together an evening seminar on the future of pensions with Piñera as the star speaker. He turned out to be a very charismatic performer, holding up his own pension book to show the audience how his fund had grown with the rising stock market.

An unexpected outcome had helped to reinforce the claims of a funded system. After just over a decade with the new system, Chile had the most equal ownership of property in all South America thanks to their pension reform. The norm in Latin America was for a small percentage of the population to own most of the wealth, but in Chile most of the wealth was owned by most of the people. This was because the pension funds to which most people belonged had invested in the companies and services privatized by the Chilean government, making their fund-holders owners of a huge chunk of the Chilean economy.

This touched on the key difference we were anxious to stress between the unfunded state system and the funded private alternatives. It was that the state system conveyed rights that depended on the policy of future governments, whereas private pension funds were property owned by their fund-holders. This property, built up over the course of a lifetime of contributions by both the fund-holder and his or her employers, could be drawn upon in retirement. It could provide income by way of interest and dividends, and the capital itself could be drawn down to some extent. Crucially, it did not die with the holder's death, but became part of the estate to be passed on in the holder's last will and testament.

It was roughly the difference between having the right to live in a subsidized state-owned house and owning that house as a capital asset which might appreciate in value and which could be bequeathed upon death. The latter sees people holding a more solid stake in the country than is entailed by a simple entitlement.

We knew we faced a hard battle in winning over the Treasury, but we persisted, returning to the subject with more seminars and studies. The problem was the transition, in that those saving up towards their own pension would also have to pay the taxes needed to honour the obligations made to current pensions and those nearing retirement. Having one generation pay twice over was never going to be popular, so we put some effort into devising other ways of funding current obligations, and of stretching the transition period over more than one generation.

We were rewarded eventually with some progress when Peter Lilley became Secretary of State for Social Security. He had been one of our Omega authors, and was a friend who regularly appeared at ASI functions. More to the point, he was convinced of the case for a funded system and asked his officials in the department to explore what options might be available. They began working with Treasury officials and put together the outlines of a policy proposal that could deal with the changeover from an unfunded system to a funded one. Perhaps at the back of their minds the Treasury team working on it realized that a huge chunk of government spending would disappear completely from future budgets if people gradually took over the provision for their own future retirement needs.

The Lilley proposal, when it emerged, was called *Basic Pensions Plus*, and looked more than forty years into the future. Governments cannot normally see beyond the next election, so this was really radical thinking. The basis of it was that there were to be two basic pensions. The familiar (and unfunded) state pension would continue for older workers and see them through their retirement. But younger workers, especially those just joining the workforce, would have an additional funded personal pension account. They would be required to save a minimum into this account, but it could be topped up with more if they wished.

This second element of their pension would be their own property, handled by an approved private provider of their choice. Because it would be invested on their behalf, it would grow roughly in line with the economy, and would represent a massive accumulation of personal wealth over the course of a working life. The basic pension, though it would continue, would represent a diminishing proportion of a person's pension over the years. Those just joining the workforce could expect to pay into their funds and watch them build up over a period of practically half a century – or even longer if they chose to continue working.

A key fact of the Lilley proposal was that the sums added up. Lilley had done a stint as financial secretary to the Treasury, and used that experience to his advantage. *Basic Pensions Plus* was fully costed and affordable, and offered the prospect of a much reduced government burden in the future. The Labour Party claimed that it would involve huge increases in government spending that would have to be met by increased taxes. Furthermore, they claimed, it posed a threat to the basic state pension itself, despite all of the commitments to the contrary.

Alas, the great pensions reform was not to be. It was approved by the Cabinet and made official government policy should it win the next election. Unfortunately it had taken nearly eighteen years to reach that position and the government's time was used up. It was not re-elected and pensions reform would have to wait until its time came again.

Soon afterwards, however, Sweden undertook a thorough-going transformation of its own pension system, privatizing it in the process and turning it into personal accounts handled by approved providers. A really innovative feature of the Swedish reform was that, while everyone was encouraged to choose a provider before the deadline date when the plan was to kick in, a default provider was set up by industry advisers in co-operation with government officials. People who had not chosen a provider by the due date were assigned to have their funds managed by the default provider.

The default provider was made to pursue a rather more cautious investment policy than the others, having a greater weighting of interest-bearing bonds as opposed to equities. Following the financial crisis which began in 2008 and saw world stock markets tumble, the default provider produced better returns for its members than those who had gone in more for equities.

The Institute decided to raise again the arguments for a funded scheme in Britain, but this time following closely along the lines which had succeeded in Sweden. This required no real change of direction, since the Swedish scheme had itself conformed quite closely to the ideas set out in *The Fortune Account*. The difference was that we now had a model closer to home in an economy as advanced as our own, and it was a successful model at that.

For its new study the ASI asked its number crunchers to calculate the amount an average person might save over the course of a working life. The assumption was that they might save 12 per cent of salary, with contributions from employers. If the long-term trend growth rate resumes over the course of the next fifty-odd years, and if people decide to work until the age of seventy-five, as they might well do in half a century's time, the result will be to make the average person reach retirement age with over a million pounds in their fund. This is measured at today's prices, not in some super-inflated funny money.

A pension system which would allow the majority to accumulate that kind of wealth over their working lives has obvious advantages over one which would have them dependent on the goodwill of future taxpayers and the competence of future governments. Furthermore, it would constitute a huge fund for potential investment in business and industry, further accelerating the wealth-creating process. The view of the ASI has been that it is only a matter of time before a government comes along that will be prepared to make so sweeping a change.

11

POLICY OVER LUNCH

The Institute pioneered a novel way of developing and putting forward its policy initiatives. We held lunches for eighteen to twenty people, usually in the St James Court or the St Ermin's Hotel, with speakers before and after the meal.

The format was always the same. Our guests would start arriving at 12 noon, to be greeted by a glass of wine in the reception room. It was a good chance for us all to meet each other and to network. At 12.30 we would open the big doors onto the dining room to reveal an oval table, laid out for the number attending, and with a cold starter already in place. After people had seated themselves and eaten the first course, the chairman, usually me, would call for order and introduce two speakers limited to ten minutes each.

There might be one token question to each and then we would all troop back through the big doors to find that the drinks had been replaced by a buffet lunch. People filled their plates and resumed their seats to find wine on the table. After the main course and dessert had been eaten, order would be called again, and two more ten-minute speeches would be given.

There might be questions and discussion over coffee, but the timing was ruthless, with the aim of enabling people to leave at 2pm.

In this way we were able to squeeze what was effectively a half-day conference with four speakers into a single lunchtime. People, such as journalists and business men and women who were notoriously short of time, found this very useful, and we were able to secure the attendance of people who would never have spared half a day. Furthermore, the ten-minute limit on speeches led our speakers to be economical when sharing their thoughts with us.

We held many of these lunchtime seminars on a variety of topics including crime, planning, buses, the environment, transport within cities and various aspects of the economy. Indeed, they came to be almost a trademark of the ASI, with a quart being squeezed into a pint pot. We asked the speakers wherever possible to give us a written version of their speech, but we recorded them all so we could transcribe those who did not do so. The talented Sylvia Meek once more showed her skills at audio typing, and changed spoken into written grammar as she did so. Those written versions would then become the chapters of a book, with Eamonn or I writing an introductory chapter to draw the ideas together.

The Institute would publish the proceedings in the form of a book with five chapters in our standard A4-size format with a glossy cover and spine. This was important because we could write the name on the spine as well as on the front, allowing its title to be read while on a bookshelf.

When we published the book, it gave us another publication and second bite at the cherry. In addition to any coverage the conference had received, we now sent out a press release with the book and received additional media coverage. It was a very cost-effective way of spreading our ideas. For the few hundred pounds it cost us to hold the lunch, and the quite low costs of editing and printing, we were able to stage a conference and issue a publication.

One such typical lunchtime seminar and subsequent publication was on the subject of funding of the arts. Eamonn gave a short introduction, then Douglas Mason spoke on 'Arts Subsidies and their Effects'. This was followed by Kingsley Amis, who spoke on 'Setting the Arts Free'. Then came Clive Wright, Esso's former manager of public affairs, covering 'The Philosophy of the Business Sponsor'. The final speaker was Professor John Pick, founding professor of the Department of Arts Policy and Management at City University, London, speaking on 'Public Funding of the Arts'.

Kingsley Amis delivered a well-reasoned elegant paper which argued that government subsidy distorted and debased artistic output and expression. He was charming and unassuming despite his formidable intellect, and fully lived up to his hard-drinking reputation. When he arrived at the pre-lunch reception and was offered 'red or white wine?' he looked dismayed, and his face sagged visibly. 'Oh,' he said plaintively, 'don't you have any real drink?' I ran down to the bar and brought him a triple Glenfiddich malt whisky, at which his face lit up. He drank two of those before the meal, and more during it. After the meal he went off in a taxi with Russell Lewis to continue drinking at the Garrick Club.

He had taken the time to prepare something special for us, which we greatly appreciated, coming from so prominent a writer. His talk was sufficiently impressive that the *Telegraph* journalist present later called us up and asked if we'd allow the paper to run it as a feature article. We agreed, of course, and they gave appropriate credits at the bottom of the article. The seminar managed to generate some coverage of the ideas and the Institute, and we later published the contributions in a book entitled *The Art of the State*, which gained even more coverage.

When we published the book and sent it out with its press release, I received a call from the features editor of the *Daily Telegraph* who asked me in high dudgeon whether we had their permission to reproduce Amis's article that they had published. 'No,' I replied, 'the *Telegraph* had *our* permission to run it.' There was a long pause and then, 'I feel such a fool.' We both laughed because it was a very easy mistake to make.

We gained hugely because we were bringing in qualified outside people to talk about their own area of expertise, like Kingsley Amis, and we were learning a great deal ourselves in the process.

We often included one or two of the MPs we were friends with and that added a little weight to our guest list. People felt they were not just exploring the subject under discussion, but were also involved in the political process through which such ideas became reality. They were helping to put new ideas into the policy process.

As with so many of our activities, it was something we tried once to break new ground, found that it worked, and then repeated the exercise. We developed it into quite a smooth routine.

12

PUBLIC HOUSES, PUBLIC LIBRARIES AND PRISONS

The ASI liked, wherever possible, to leaven its theory with a dollop of practice. A policy proposal was more likely to be taken seriously if a version of it had been tried elsewhere. This gave legislators and civil servants the chance to see how it had worked in reality, and perhaps to learn from any mistakes that had been made.

In the case of licensing laws covering the sale of alcoholic beverages, there were examples of different approaches applied in different parts of the world. They ranged from a very lax 'anything goes' policy to tight regulation, with alcoholic drinks only available from state outlets during specified hours.

The laws in England governing public houses were quite strict. Limited hours were set by law and many tourists visiting Britain were puzzled to find when they went to buy another drink that the deadline for doing so had already passed. In general on weekdays the legal hours were between 11am and 10.30pm, with an afternoon break between 3pm and 5.30pm. London and a few other places fared slightly better, with an extra half hour at night. It was tighter on Sundays and some religious holidays, with hours limited to between 12 noon and 2pm, and then from 7pm to 10.30pm.

The origins of this tight regulation were various attempts to curb public drunkenness in previous centuries. The most stringent controls had come in during the First World War to prevent munitions workers arriving inebriated at their factories. Circumstances and the pace of life had changed, and many people resented what seemed like pointless and arbitrary restrictions.

Douglas Mason, who wrote many of our Scottish papers, volunteered to write a report for us, and researched it thoroughly. He had a ready-made example from within the UK. Scotland had been stricter in its application of licensing laws, but had become more liberal following the Errol Report. Its 1976 reform had transferred licensing power from Justices of the Peace to local authority boards made up of councillors. Thus Scotland had gone from having much stricter controls than England to having much more lax ones. And there had been time to observe the results.

Douglas' report for the Adam Smith Institute, *Time to Call Time*, collated some telling evidence. The architect of the Scottish reforms, Dr Christopher Clayson, had pointed out that prior to 1976, 'in every index for studying the misuse of alcohol, the Scots were worse than the English. Personal or family drink problems, breaches of the peace, drunkenness and drunk driving were all two or three times as bad in Scotland.' So were alcohol-related psychiatric disorders and illnesses.

This was despite the fact that Scotland and England paid the same taxes on drink, had similar incomes, spent the same on alcohol and had similar proportions of teetotallers and heavy drinkers. Following the Scottish liberalization, all of these adverse measures showed significant reductions. Scotland, which had fared worse than England when its alcohol laws were tighter, now fared better. The extension of hours had led to fewer alcohol-related problems, not more as some had predicted.

It was a very convincing case and generated a great deal of coverage when it was released. Douglas himself was widely interviewed in newspapers and on radio and television. He was even invited on a speaking tour of Australia to cover the subject at a hotel industry conference, and coped with his lifelong fear of flying in order to accept it. Never having flown, he had little idea of the ancillary costs associated with it, and when I flew into Hawaii to rendezvous I found him waiting in my hotel lobby literally penniless!

He drank only sweet cider himself, so had no axe to grind for the alcohol lobby or the big brewers and distillers. As a libertarian he thought that people should be able to drink what and when they wanted to, provided they did no harm to others.

When liberalization was proposed in England, a chorus of voices warned that it would lead to a rise in all of the alcohol-related problems. The ASI case that not only had this not happened in Scotland, but the reverse had happened, was convincing evidence and argument against this point of view. The liberalization case won through and the English laws were made more liberal.

While the great majority of people have enjoyed their new freedoms and chosen to enjoy drink in a less hurried and more relaxed atmosphere, there seems to have been a rise in binge drinking by young people in city centres. Despite calls by some for tighter restrictions on drinking hours and steep rises in the taxes levied on alcohol, most studies see the problem as a cultural one rather than one which might be solved by making it harder and more expensive to obtain alcohol. In many other countries where alcohol is as widely available and as cheap, people seem able to enjoy it without bingeing. Some studies note that it seems to be an issue with northern countries and may have deep cultural roots.

The ASI on several occasions opposed the tendency of governments to use the drinks industry as a cash cow to raise revenue, while covering itself by referring to the medical impact of alcohol. The ASI's case was that most health problems derive from excessive drinking, which most people do not do, and that it is the heavy drinkers who are least deterred by price rises. They just trade down for cheaper ways of obtaining alcohol.

Several times the ASI came out against increases in duties on alcohol, arguing that this was punishing ordinary citizens for the excesses of a few, it was unlikely to be effective as a deterrent and would cause more people to buy drink abroad rather than pay the high UK taxes. We argued that it would not even raise the extra revenue that was predicted.

One of the Institute's neatest publications on the subject was a research paper by Dr Paul Haines of the University of St Andrews. He argued that excise duties on alcohol discriminated against whisky in particular by hitting it harder than the levies it imposed on such things as beer, cider and wine. He advocated a simpler, fairer tax that would simply be imposed on products per litre of alcohol, regardless of the type of drink involved.

The Institute published his work under the title *Freedom An' Whisky Gang Thegither*, with a picture on the cover of the book showing the statue of liberty holding a shot glass instead of the more familiar torch. The ASI regarded this as an opportunity to point to the anomalies and absurdities of excise duties and taxes on alcohol, as well as striking a blow in favour of a very successful and very famous Scottish industry. Once again we were making a gesture in the direction of our St Andrews and Scottish backgrounds

LIBRARIES

The ASI suffered a rather more hostile reception to its proposals on public libraries. Once again it was the prolific and hard-working Douglas Mason who did the research. He established that the overwhelming borrowing from free public libraries was of popular blockbuster novels, modern romantic fiction, and coming in a distant third were do-it-yourself books. His case was that this was not what public libraries were supposed to be about. Many had been established in Victorian days from a belief that ordinary people who could not afford to buy books should be able to have free access to them on loan, in the hope of encouraging self-education.

More than a few modern libraries had diversified into loaning from a collection of popular music records or DVDs. They were severely constrained by their budgets and many had a very small allowance from which to add to their stocks.

The case Douglas was making was that if they were to make a small charge (he was talking of pennies) for their popular fiction, this would generate revenue for them to continue their operations and add to their stocks. The Institute duly published his report, *Ex Libris*, and the storm broke. I don't suppose it helped that our rather classical cover depicted one of the muses with a book on her lap, head in hands with a look of despair.

The proposal certainly received wide coverage. The media realized that this would probably outrage the arts brigade, just as our proposal to withdraw state funding for the arts had done, and featured it in many interviews and stories. We were all careful to stress that any charges would not apply to children, students, unemployed people and retired people, and would not apply to any books that might be deemed broadly educational.

The argument against seemed to be that the proposal amounted to vandalism on a grand scale. The claim was that people who began by reading popular fiction by Barbara Cartland might move on to Thucydides, and would be deterred from even starting down that road if they had to pay a few pennies for each book borrowed.

The abuse was as widespread as the misrepresentation. In fairness, I do not suppose that any of our celebrity critics had read our report, and were going only on press reports that omitted many of the important details. Alan Bennett saw Eamonn on BBC's *Newsnight* and described him as 'a nylon under-panted figure', though I think this was just speculation. In his diaries he reports how depressed he was that someone like me could advocate closing down public libraries, and on another occasion referred to me as 'Madsen Pirie, also from the Adam Smith Institute for the criminally insane'.

I tried to redress this kind of reaction by pointing out in interviews that my local public library had featured in most of my teenage years, and that my bicycle had been regularly parked outside it on school-free afternoons. Nowhere did we suggest that libraries should be closed. Alas, the received wisdom is that all our services must be free or the army of philistines will be clamouring at our gates.

Douglas himself was a great bibliophile. He had one of Britain's biggest collections of science fiction books. His Glenrothes house had bookshelves built onto every wall, even the stair landings, and was completely lined with books where others might have used wallpaper. He dealt part time in antiquarian and rare books, and loved the smell and feel of their bindings. His report on public libraries was by no means a philistine attack.

The Alan Bennett criticism was disappointing, not least because I regard him as one of the greatest playwrights of recent times, and find both his fiction and his diaries full of the conviction and elegance of style that marks out a truly great talent. The other celebrities and columnists who attacked us mattered much less to us, and they were in any case criticizing what they thought we had said, rather than what we had actually said.

We certainly did not want to close libraries then, nor later when local governments were faced with the need for economies and found it easier to save money by closing libraries and swimming pools than dispensing with the services of bureaucrats. The ASI's case was then, and has been since, that we should not assume that a publicly funded free supply is the only model that can be considered. Modest charges for more commercial items, or contracting out libraries to be run in more efficient and up-to-date ways by outside agencies should also be tried, as should co-operative community ventures in which a few professionals co-ordinate an army of volunteers.

In his account Douglas had pointed to philanthropic libraries and commercial libraries run by shops. Bookshops were already adding coffee bars to attract customers, so why, he asked, could public libraries not be integrated with other activities and services? He thought that other models should be tried and tested to see if they might make public libraries more viable, and more capable of surviving into the modern world.

PRISONS

Peter Young, now back from the United States, at our request had made a study of the US prisons whose operation had been contracted out to the private sector. Now he examined the over-extended and outdated UK prison system and concluded that this type of privatization could be hugely beneficial.

America's privately run prisons were less expensive to run, but while saving money was an attractive way to interest government, it was not the point of the exercise. The point was that in the US the privately run prisons were better on just about every measure that could be examined.

Typically a private contractor would build a new prison, or

in some cases reconfigure a state-run prison, so that it could be operated by fewer staff. They were designed to give staff a greater view of what was happening. Typically the conditions within cells were improved and humanized, giving the inmates less of a sense of alienation. Their staff were trained to operate a more relaxed environment, wearing sweatshirts or tracksuits instead of the more intimidating prison uniforms that characterized the federal or state operations.

What was remarkable about the private prisons were the statistics which measured their success. Their average rate of assaults on staff or other prisoners was lower. The rate of suicide or attempted suicide was lower. There were fewer mental problems and physical illnesses. Drug use was lower. On virtually every measure they outperformed the publicly operated prisons.

The most telling figure of all was that they had a lower rate of recidivism following release. Many of the firms had bonus clauses written into their contracts based on how many released inmates stayed free of crime for a least two years following release. This motivated them to undertake educational and job-training programmes for their inmates to make them less likely to be drawn back into crime afterwards.

Peter produced a report we published as *The Prison Cell* (many of our titles contained puns). It recommended handing over some of Britain's prisons to private contractors on a trial basis, and having at least one new prison wholly built and operated by a private firm.

The report caused some consternation because some commentators thought we were getting close to handing out one of the core justice functions of state to the private sector. The book made it clear that this was not the case. Prosecution, trial, conviction and sentencing were not affected. These would still be done by the judicial system, but the actual administration of a prison sentence would be carried out by those under contract to the state instead of those paid directly by the state.

One grey area was identified: any remission of sentence for good behaviour would be based on the judgement of those running the prison. They would not have the power to reduce the sentence themselves, but their recommendation would go forward to the body that did make that decision. In our eyes this presented no problem. Sentencing already occasionally took account of the opinions and reports of people not directly employed by the state.

The book provoked some interest in the Home Office. The prospect of achieving more effective and humane prison conditions while simultaneously saving money was good enough to merit close inspection. The prison system was thought to be creaking at capacity and here was the promise of securing more without spending extra resources.

The Home Office telephoned to order some copies of the report. They asked for its full title, so I told them it was called *The Prison Cell*, adding 'that last word is spelled with a C'. I was rewarded by a laugh at the other end of the phone.

However, we were up against some serious, and indeed intimidating, opposition from prison officers. A powerful union to whom no government was willing to stand up, they ran the prison system pretty much as they wanted and, as ex-lags who told their stories to us confirmed, the system was run very much for the prison officers' convenience, however inhumane and humiliating that was for prisoners and however counterproductive it was in terms of prisoners being properly engaged and led down the path of rehabilitation.

Peter Young had direct experience of their thuggery when he appeared on *Newsnight* to discuss the proposal, with one of the union's bosses on the other side. Peter, armed with facts and figures about the practical success of private prisons in other countries, won the argument pretty easily. On the way out of the studio, however, the prison officer union official squared up to him and said, threateningly, 'Right, we know who you are. Maybe you will never end up in custody, but if you ever do, you'd better watch out. We've got your name.' Peter was still shaking the next morning when he related the incident to us. But the event simply strengthened our belief that Britain's prison system was rotten and needed the most fundamental reform.

Studies were commissioned and junior ministers went on inspection tours of private prisons in the US. A parliamentary committee sent some of its members on a fact-finding visit on the strength of our report and its findings. Eventually the Home Office took on board the idea and announced that some UK prisons would be operated by private contractors on a trial basis. They based the contracts on some of those drawn up for handling private prisons in the US.

There was one minor hiccup involving the use of private contractors to transfer prisoners from prisons or police cells for court appearances. There was a series of escapes by prisoners from the custody of a private security firm, Group 4, and the press played it up as though the firm was unfit. Spokesmen on behalf of the Prison Officers Association did not pass up the opportunity to attack the private sector. It was a brief storm in a teacup, however, and died down when figures established that escapes from private security firms during transfers were in fact fewer than those from the state's officers.

13

MEDIA COVERAGE AND *ENLIGHTENMENT* IDEAS

We understood from the start that we would need a high media profile if we were to talk to our target audience in public. We needed to have our ideas covered in the press and by the electronic media. Fortunately we had already done one important thing by sheer chance. We had chosen a name that began with an 'A'. Journalists tended to keep lists of their contacts, and if they wanted to phone someone for a comment they often started at the top with Adam Smith Institute. We used to joke that if we were doing it over again, we'd have called it the Aaron Institute just to make sure. As it was, we received many phone calls from the media every week asking us for comments.

We knew by instinct that what the media valued was brevity and accuracy. They wanted a sound-bite or a pithy quote, but one that reached to the heart of the matter. We became adept at saying what we wanted to say on radio or television in forty-second slots, and in replying to newspaper journalists with two-sentence answers.

As our publications attracted more attention, we found ourselves invited to appear on public service programmes, including *Newsnight* and Radio 4's *Today* programme. Often there would be a brief slot about our latest publication, then an interview to answer questions put by the presenter or a brief debate with someone opposed to the ideas it represented.

The most terrifying of all was *Question Time*, the weekly TV panel discussion in front of a live audience. It had (and still has) a huge audience. I have appeared on it three times, and took each one very seriously. We brought cameras and video recorders to our office and went through some of the questions that might come up that week.

On the first appearance, by sheer chance, five of our friends had managed to obtain tickets before they even knew I would be on it. This meant I at least had some friends in the audience. They had the good sense to scatter themselves throughout the audience so they would not appear as a tiny group when they wanted to applaud anything.

The point about *Question Time* is that while it is fundamentally an entertainment programme about public events, it is one watched by most people involved in politics. It was the only one for which people would recognize me in the streets or in shops on days the following it. What made it so terrifying was the thought of making a gaffe before so large an audience.

THE *ENLIGHTENMENT* SERIES

In order to save the cost of so many publications and conferences, the ASI tried to put forward policy ideas in the form of unaccompanied press releases. We attempted this a few times but stopped even trying when we found that the media were not covering them. If there were a book, report or paper alongside the press release, or if a minister had made a speech at one of our conferences, this was regarded as news, but unadorned ideas did not fit the media's perception of a news item.

We decided that the minimum that would 'count' as a publication would probably be a sheet of A3 paper folded to make four sides and printed with double columns under a suitably impressive heading. It had the added advantage that we could produce it relatively quickly, as well as cheaply, and it would increase our ability to put ideas out into the public domain.

The name we chose for it was the *Adam Smith Enlightenment*, with a candle flame as its logo. This was a nod to the Scottish Enlightenment, the movement of Scottish intelligentsia of which Adam Smith had been one of the leaders. By putting out several such papers per year with new and newsworthy policy initiatives, we hoped the media would become familiar with its format and treat its ideas as worthy of a news mention. It was a continuation of our strategy of talking to influential people through the media.

HOTOL

One of the first ones we did was a paper supporting the development of HOTOL (Horizontal Take-Off and Landing), a proposed aerospace vehicle that would use air-breathing engines in the atmosphere, moving to full rocket power to take it into orbit. It was unmanned and constituted a way of putting satellites into orbit at very low cost compared with conventional rocket launches. It was designed to take off and land on conventional runways.

Of course, the technology acquired in developing such a vehicle could be applied to other advanced projects, with great advantages for the UK aerospace industry. It would give Britain a space programme on the cheap, and might serve as the basis for the subsequent development of hypersonic intercontinental passenger carriers and perhaps eventually even a manned space programme.

We used to speculate about its possible role as an intercontinental carrier, saying that you could get from London to Sydney in just three hours, of which two would be spent getting through the airports.

At the back of our minds, however, were the potential military uses of such a vehicle and our suggestion was that some of the development costs might be met from the UK defence budget. The US Strategic Defense Initiative proposed by President Reagan would certainly find uses for the technology behind such a vehicle and it might be a way of having Britain included in that initiative.

To our relief the paper did receive some coverage, perhaps because there was a nice artist's impression of HOTOL in flight that made good newspaper copy. It showed that our new *Enlightenment* format worked, where a simple unaccompanied press release did not.

THE LOTTERY

One of the *Enlightenment* papers that attracted a great deal of attention was the one proposing a national lottery. Denis Vaughan, the orchestral conductor, wrote an article in the *Sunday Telegraph* proposing a national lottery to help fund the arts in Britain. We approached Denis and asked if he would write a short paper for us on the subject. He accepted with alacrity, seizing the chance to develop his idea and bring it more attention.

Other countries, notably Spain, had national lotteries, as did several US states. The funds raised were used for a variety of purposes including, sometimes, government revenues. We wanted something more focused, so the proposal was for a national lottery that would fund 'good causes', principally the arts and sport and some medical and other charities. Sport was added to broaden the numbers who would receive benefit from the lottery fund. The lottery would come under the auspices of government, which would appoint a body to distribute the receipts.

The advantage of a lottery is that it is voluntary: no one has to buy a ticket and those who do can dream of the chances of winning millions. Extra money is raised that taxpayers might not be willing to support if it came from taxation.

The *Enlightenment* paper proposing a national lottery attracted much interest. The arts brigade, large numbers of whom we had offended by calling for withdrawal of state funding for the arts and having libraries charge small amounts for popular fiction, were broadly in support, seeing the chance to bring in extra funds that might not otherwise be possible.

The popular press liked the idea of large numbers having a flutter every week with the chance of winning millions, and sporting organizations liked the prospect of funding for sports clubs and academies. The only groups really opposed were religious groups who were against gambling *per se*, and the football pools companies. The latter recognized correctly that a national lottery would take away a significant portion of their market, diverting to good causes the gambling money that was presently going to augment their profits.

Denis himself was a tireless advocate, doing interviews and writing articles, and briefing MPs and ministers. The national lottery was adopted as government policy and the enabling legislation passed by Parliament.

The distribution of lottery receipts was remarkable. Of every £1 spent on tickets, 50p went into the prize fund. Of the remaining 50p, 28p was assigned to good causes, 12p in government duty, 5p to retailers as commission and 4.5p in operating costs to Camelot with 0.5p as their profit. It returned to good causes a higher proportion of each £1 than any other official lottery. It is reckoned to have increased funding for the arts and sport sevenfold.

The main criticism of the National Lottery is that the tickets are mostly bought by lower-income people, whereas a significant proportion of the arts institutions that benefit are those enjoyed by people on much higher incomes. I took the view that rather too much lottery money went to fund the Royal Opera House at Covent Garden, when it might have been more appropriate to allocate more funds to local arts ventures such as repertory companies and youth orchestras. As it was, some commented that it taxed the poor to subsidize the enjoyment of the rich.

This is less true of sports institutions, however, and large numbers of low- and middle-income people have benefitted from the support for sports and the medical and other charities that are included among the good causes. And of course players gain something from the excitement of thinking that their numbers might come up next time, and that they might join the over 2,500 millionaires that the National lottery has already created.

I suggested to John Major at one stage that each welfare recipient should get a free weekly lottery ticket to give them a chance to dream of riches, and to take them off the welfare rolls if they won. The Prime Minister was intrigued by the idea but his officials killed it straight away, claiming that the lobbies representing poor people would demand the money instead of the ticket. The cost of free tickets could have been absorbed by slightly diluting the chances of winning, but to add the cash price of a ticket to every welfare recipient would have been very costly.

OTHER *ENLIGHTENMENT* PAPERS

The ASI used the same format several times, always to float a new idea and put it into the public domain. Two very bright young academics, Nigel Allington and Nicholas O'Shaughnessy, became regular contributors. They wrote a very good paper for us explaining how the BBC might be changed from a fundamentally statist organization into something more in tune with the way worldwide communications had been developing.

The BBC seemed to be obsessed with the idea that it had to do everything. It felt it had to compete with Independent Television for popular audiences for sports fixtures and mass light entertainment. It seemed bizarre that these should be supported out of taxation when ITV managed to provide this kind of fare without subsidies from taxpayers.

The BBC had made what we thought was a wrong decision to justify its licence fee by mass viewing figures. It thought that if it abandoned the mass market to its private competitors, it would lose credibility and the justification for its licence fee. We thought the opposite – that the BBC's justification was that it provided broadcasting fare that might be difficult to finance on a commercial basis. We suggested that popular programmes such as BBC1, Radio 1 and Radio 2 might be financed by advertising, as their commercial counterparts already were. Indeed, they could be privatized and survive quite happily on their ability to attract audiences without taxpayer support. The BBC's more serious channels might be turned into subscription services instead of being financed from central taxation.

We took the view that the BBC's justification was public service broadcasting. Even here, we suggested that other companies might be invited to bid to provide public service programmes. Our two young academics produced a good paper setting out how the BBC might be restructured and we were happy to publish it in the *Enlightenment* series.

We had our own problems with the BBC and its inbuilt bias. Too often its commentators would refer to us as 'the right-wing Adam Smith Institute'. Left-wing bodies would be referred to without an opposite description. They were 'independent', or at worst 'centre left'. The problem was that the BBC also used the term 'right wing' to refer to hard-line communists, fascists, US extremists, the British National Party and anything unpleasant. The ASI was libertarian, not remotely authoritarian as the term 'right wing' implied. We suggested mischievously that they probably employed someone full time to insert the adjective 'right wing' whenever the words 'Adam Smith Institute' were used.

We regularly complained to producers, but it had no effect until we began to say just before an interview that if we were described as 'the right-wing Adam Smith Institute', we would correct it live on air. Several times the presenters would then delete the offending words from their introductory script, and eventually the message must have got through.

Nigel Allington and Nicholas O'Shaughnessy were very productive. It was as we were publishing their third paper that I asked them why they did it. After all, I pointed out, it took time and effort and we did not pay them. The answer from one of them was revealing: 'Madsen, you don't really understand academic life. We work for a year and a half to produce a scholarly paper. It appears in an obscure journal and is read by maybe twelve people, of whom seven don't understand it. We publish a paper with the Adam Smith Institute and we appear in the newspapers. We are interviewed on radio and TV. It's worth it for the looks of sheer hatred we receive as we walk through the staff common room!'

The real answer was, of course, that, like all our writers, they did it because it advanced a cause they believed in. We did not pay our writers because we couldn't afford to. We made an exception in the case of freelance writers who made their living by writing, but even then we paid only a small fee, as much as we could reasonably afford. Authors usually wrote for us without reward because they wanted to have people listen to their ideas.

The *Enlightenment* series ran for a few years before everything moved online, generating papers on privatizing the Post Office,

Europe's Common Agricultural Policy, tax simplification, spreading self-employment and allowing solicitors the right of audience in courts. This was in addition to several editions supporting or extending policy proposals we had already made in more weighty reports. The *Enlightenment* papers represented a good and inexpensive way of keeping an idea in the public mind.

14

REVISING RATES

From the late 1970s and early 1980s there was a rising level of discontent about the rates, which were the property taxes used to provide some of the finance for local government services. One complaint was that not enough people paid them. In some areas the council house tenants outnumbered home-owners and could vote for high spending local councils who would jack up the rates for those who had not voted for them. Douglas Mason calculated that in Scotland only one in six adults actually paid the rates, allowing the other five to vote for high-tax services without concern.

There were complaints about the business rate, too. There was no longer a business vote, but businesses still paid rates. Left-wing local authorities commonly chose to raise the business rates in order to provide services that might attract voters. In some urban areas businesses had either closed down because they could not afford the burden, or had voted with their feet and gone somewhere more amenable to business.

This could create a downward spiral. As businesses left, the local authorities further increased the business rate to finance their spending from those that remained. The increases caused yet more businesses to leave, leaving some urban areas as devastated waste-lands. Victor Serebriakoff, the President of Mensa who took part in our activities over many years, described the phenomenon of 'social black holes, from which nothing emerged, not even light'.

Ratable values, which determined the tax level, were only adjusted at many year intervals, leading to anomalies and injustices. They were calculated on imputed rental value, which made the figures pretty arbitrary and meaningless since so few properties were rented. A new ratable value adjustment caused a storm of protest.

The pressure was building for government to come up with a solution. Since rates were seen to be an increasingly urgent problem, it is quite likely that several people, including those in government, were working on possible alternatives, and might have come up with similar ideas. I first heard of the idea of a local poll tax (which we called a *per capita* tax) to replace the rates from Douglas Mason. I was visiting St Andrews and met him in Rufflets Hotel on the edge of town. He had drawn on his own experience as a local councillor and decided that a flat-rate local tax would be superior in many ways to the rates system.

The *Daily Mail* had asked me that morning to write a feature article that might offer some hope to beleaguered rate-payers, so I asked Douglas to map out the essentials of his suggestion. When the article appeared it attracted some favourable comment, so Douglas incorporated the proposal into the *Omega Report on Local Government*, which he was editing, and filled it out in greater detail in a paper for us entitled *Revising the Rating System*.

By this time the idea was in circulation and several people had been working on different versions of it, but the fundamental argument was that local government services were more about services than they were about government. We should not really be engaging in politics to get our streets swept and our dustbins emptied. At the heart of this was our treatment of people as consumers of government as well as participants in it. This idea was later to find expression in the Citizen's Charter.

Rich people should pay more taxes than poor people because they can afford to, but that does not mean they should pay more for their milk or their bread. We treated many local services as consumer items which should be charged for just as private services were. It was thought fairer if those who received the services should be the ones paying for them. Everyone is less careful about how they spend other people's money, and it was thought that if people knew they were the ones who would be paying, they would be less likely to vote in profligate and high-spending councils.

Douglas had some important caveats in his writings on the subject. Firstly, he suggested that local expenditure should be frozen for the years just before and after the changeover, to prevent councils using the confusion of the transition to sneak in big spending increases, as the infamous 'decimal diddlers' had used the currency change to raise prices back in 1971. Douglas also stipulated that the charge should not be levied on those who could not pay it. Students, together with the unemployed, should not be charged, or should be sent a charge notice marked 'paid by taxpayers' to let them know that public services were not actually produced without someone having to fund them.

There was a long national debate on the subject as William Waldegrave piloted the proposal. Tory conferences backed it overwhelmingly. When a version of the proposal became government policy, those caveats Douglas had stipulated were not incorporated. It was introduced first in Scotland, which had the Scots screaming that their country was being used as a test bed. Had it been introduced second in Scotland no doubt they would have claimed the Scots were being left behind. And if it had been introduced at the same time, perhaps the charge might have been that once again the government was failing to recognize the essential difference between England and Scotland.

The government also took control of the business rate and had it set nationally. This was done to protect local businesses from councils that might keep taxes on business high in order to reduce the burden that fell on their electors.

When Douglas first put forward his proposal, he calculated the average per capita charge would be roughly the level of the annual motor vehicle licence plus the annual BBC TV licence, both of them also poll taxes where everyone paid the same. However, over the time it took for the changeover to be enacted and implemented, local spending in many areas had gone through the roof, and the average would now be several times that amount. The version that the Thatcher government actually introduced did not exclude students and those on benefit, either. Critics quickly dubbed it the 'poll tax', and harked back to Richard II's failure.

When the new system came into effect in England there were violent protests similar to those that happened two decades later over the increase in university fees. The English, unlike the French, were not used to vandalism, arson, and attacks on public buildings and on the police as part of political protest. The English were more into peaceful marches, and the 'poll tax' violence shocked many people then, as did student violence twenty years later.

Douglas claimed that in its second year in Scotland the tax was starting to achieve the intended effects, and that people living under high-spending councils were beginning to vote for more moderate candidates. I never saw the figures, but it would not have mattered anyway. Margaret Thatcher had won three elections in a row, but had now lost the confidence of her Cabinet (mainly on European issues it seemed) and could not continue as Prime Minister.

Her departure led to the immediate replacement of the poll tax by a new Council Tax, which was really a variant of the old rating system. People had to pay the new tax according to the value of the property they lived in. Michael Heseltine, one of Margaret Thatcher's biggest critics, had a hand in the replacement proposals. They were an unhappy compromise. One idea was to raise some of the finances of local government through an increase in the VAT on fuel, but that disappeared along the way.

Looking back with the advantage of hindsight, there were several things wrong with the tax and the way in which it was implemented. Firstly, there were the two caveats Douglas had mentioned. Had local council expenditure been frozen, there would not have been the shock of such large bills landing on the doormat. Had students and those on benefit been exempt, the charges of unfairness might have been more muted.

There were, however, more serious structural flaws with the poll tax which should guide any future reform of local authority finance. The tax came all at once in an annual bill, meaning that people had to save up in order to be able to pay it. The Council Tax that replaced it overcame this to some extent by widespread use of direct debit payments to spread the tax over several monthly payments. Direct debit was much less widely used at the time of the poll tax, so this had not been an option.

More seriously, the tax did not take place on transactions. No taxes are good, but the least offensive ones are attached to an income or spending stream, diverting a little of it in taxation. An income tax has an earning stream; a sales tax has a spending stream; the same applies to profits taxes or duties on alcohol, tobacco or petrol. But the poll tax was on people, not attached to any transaction.

The Council Tax suffers the same drawback, in that it is measured by the value of properties, most of which have no income stream.

There was one final and serious flaw in the structure of the poll tax: there was no one to collect it. Government collects many of its taxes by using its citizens as unpaid civil servants. Employers collect PAYE income tax from their employees. Sales assistants collect the excise duty on cigarettes; publicans collect it on beer and whisky. Supermarkets and shops collect it on wine and the other alcoholic drinks they sell. VAT is collected by businesses.

In all of these cases government compels others to perform its work of tax collection. In the case of the poll tax there were no transactions involving such people so local government had to collect the tax itself. That meant it needed a body of people in its employ who could put together a new database, calculate what was due, send out the bills and pursue any transgressors. It was both cumbersome and expensive, as well as not being very efficient.

In retrospect, given all of these disadvantages, the option should probably have been for a local sales tax. These work routinely in most US states. They are collected by shop assistants whose tills do the work for them. Most people do not mind paying a little extra with each transaction and their tax liability is thus spread over a year's purchases. As Americans say, they nickel and dime their local taxes instead of facing a large bill all at once.

In the UK there might be boundary problems, as there are on some US state borders, where people who live in one authority make many of their purchases in another. If this encouraged local authorities to be more efficient and less profligate, to avoid driving their taxpayers to buy elsewhere, this might be no bad thing.

Douglas Mason always regretted that the poll tax had not been given the chance to bed itself in and smooth out some of the flaws.

He described it 'like killing a baby because it hasn't yet developed into an adult'. Douglas himself developed brain cancer in the years after these events. He gradually deteriorated and finally died in December 2004. He received obituaries in most papers and was referred to by some as the 'father of the poll tax'. He was also acclaimed as one of the backroom boys of the Thatcher revolution and many of the papers covered the contributions he had made to the work of the Adam Smith Institute.

15

TAX FREEDOM DAY

The ASI did not invent Tax Freedom Day. When we took up the idea in Britain it was already done by one or two US think tanks, most notably the Tax Foundation based in Boston. The strongest claim for the originator of the idea suggests that it was Dallas Hostetler, a businessman based in Florida, who in 1948 came up with a neat way to calculate the financial burden that government imposed on its citizens.

The Adam Smith Institute took up the idea in the UK, and began to calculate Tax Freedom Day every year and publish the results. The methodology is straightforward. We take the total of taxes paid by citizens. Obviously this includes income tax and VAT. It also includes the excise duties on petrol, drink and tobacco. It includes taxes on business, too, because these are ultimately paid by individuals who buy the goods or services which business produces.

We include all kinds of obscure taxes such as those on insurance and air tickets. National Insurance is properly included, since it is a tax by any other name. The sweep includes everything that goes to the Exchequer, and also the taxes that go to local government. In other words all tax is included.

The next step is to calculate the Net National Income (NNI), which is for these purposes a rather better measure than Gross Domestic Product (GDP). We then calculate the percentage of NNI (which is effectively the nation's income) taken by government, and express this as a percentage of the year. Thus if the government's take amounts to 40 per cent of NNP, we calculate 40 per cent of the year, which comes in a normal year to 146 days. The 147th day of the year is then declared to be Tax Freedom Day.

The idea is that if you start work on 1 January and pay everything you earn to the government, after 146 days the average person will have paid off all the taxes they pay to the government that year. From then on the rest of the year is yours, and the money you earn from then on will be your own. That is why it is called Tax Freedom Day. In some years it has been less than 40 per cent that has gone to government, but in some years it has been more.

The actual calculations were done for us over many years by Gabriel Stein, an international economist from Sweden now domiciled in the UK and working with Lombard Street Research. After the budget each year he would crunch the numbers, make his projections and come up not only with a figure, but with a commentary to accompany it.

The Institute has published Tax Freedom Day every year as a way of exposing and dramatizing the proportion of the wealth we create taken by government. Many people look at the income tax they pay and do not fully appreciate how much additional tax they pay in a variety of ways. The advantage of Tax Freedom Day is that it is an overall figure that measures everything the government takes.

The very first time we did this, we discovered the media liked it. Tax Freedom Day is an event that resonates. Most people like to grumble about taxes, especially when they have been rising, and Tax Freedom Day provides a focus. The papers usually cover it in a short couple of paragraphs, drawing attention to whether it has come earlier in the year (meaning a lower share to government), or later (meaning a higher share).

The local radio stations regarded it as an ideal peg for phone-in programmes in the morning. 'Guess what today is, folks? It's your tax freedom day. You've paid off your taxes for the year. But everything you've done since New Year's Day has been for the government. It's taken until early June…'

We were entirely happy to go on these programmes, either from a studio or over the phone, and join in the general moaning about how taxes were too high. Behind it was the very serious point that high taxes eroded Britain's competitive standing internationally, leading companies to start up and expand in more tax-friendly jurisdictions. All taxes impede the wealth-creating process and, in general, the higher the taxes the more they do this.

Each year, on Tax Freedom Day the updated accounts of previous years were published, taking account of any base changes the government had introduced, and correcting for inflation. It enabled people to see the steady advance of government over the years. It was not remorseless, though: during a decade mostly under Margaret Thatcher's premiership, the government share had declined or stayed the same for ten years in a row. Since then it has risen fairly steadily.

Gordon Brown hated Tax Freedom Day when he was Chancellor of the Exchequer. He prided himself on his great cleverness in concealing taxes so they did not show and people did not realize they were paying them. They just found out that they were poorer than they had expected to be and were not sure why. These were the infamous 'stealth taxes' that were finally exposed. People cottoned on to his methods and started reading the small print of his budget – the things he had not announced in his speeches.

Always there were new taxes hidden away, even when he claimed to be cutting taxes.

The ASI was very opposed to stealth taxes because they cheapen the relationship between citizens and their government. Taxes should be open and acknowledged so that citizens know their obligations. Taxpayers might grumble, but it is a more honest relationship than one which tricks money out of their pockets without their knowing about it.

Because Tax Freedom Day counts overall taxes from all sources, it sweeps even the stealth taxes into its calculations and exposes what the government is doing. Gordon Brown then switched to borrowing, so that it would appear that he was not raising taxes. Borrowing is, of course, deferred taxation in that it has to be paid off sooner or later. Rather than make it appear that he was bringing Tax Freedom Day earlier in the year, we started factoring borrowing into the calculations.

Chancellors of all parties and complexions do not like Tax Freedom Day because it reveals the size of what government is taking and makes people more likely to complain about it. To us that is part of its success and justification. Gordon Brown liked it less than other Chancellors because it exposed what I believe to be his fundamental dishonesty. And the Treasury never liked it because it exposed the real level of the tax burden, but it always resonated with the general public.

We started to market Tax Freedom Day, not by simply sending out the booklet and press release, but adding gimmicks to draw attention to it. One year Eamonn posed for photographs with a ball and chain to emphasize the burden taxpayers were carrying. Another year we sent out mouse-mats with key facts and figures about Tax Freedom Day, present and past. Always we would dramatize a few 'gee whiz' figures that emphasized the enormity of our tax and debt burden.

Tax Freedom Day in the UK was always compared with those of other countries. Britain in the 1970s had been an international joke, with a top tax rate of income tax of 83 per cent, rising to 98 per cent if it were from investment income. In the 1980s Britain's position had been reversed, turning it into a low-tax country that was a good place to do business. Tax Freedom Day tracked those changes over the years. We enjoyed a good relationship with Nigel Lawson when he was Chancellor, in that he made it his policy to lower taxes in every budget and always to abolish at least one tax.

Alas, that enviable position was itself subsequently reversed. Years of high spending, government profligacy and stealth taxes turned Britain, once again, into a high-tax country that business is more likely to move out of than into. In the coming years Tax Freedom Day will have much to do.

16

THE HEALTH OF NATIONS

After the privatization of most of the state industries and utilities, the Institute concentrated increasingly on the state services of health, education and welfare. Our approach on pensions was for individual Fortune Accounts to support fully funded retirement pensions. On state schooling it was the 'virtual voucher' outlined in the *Omega Report on Education*. This combined independence for schools with free parental choice between them, and the state funding following the child to the chosen school.

Health presented a difficult problem. There could be no question of privatizing the National Health Service in the way in which the telephone service or the gas industry had been privatized. Yet there was no way in which the NHS could be left as it was. The anomalies of its structure meant that it was coming apart at the seams. Hospitals were often over-crowded and unpleasant, and in some cases unhygienic. Waiting lists were long and lengthening. The recovery rates for various categories of illness were falling behind those of other advanced countries.

The NHS operated as a top-down system, controlled and funded from the centre, and it was literally too big to manage. The story at the time was that it was the world's third largest organization, following only the Red Army in China and the Indian State Railway. This might have depended on how these things were counted, but there was no escaping the size of the NHS, or its claim on the national budget of the UK.

The NHS was subject to practically none of the forces and influences which make private business more efficient, more competitive and more ready to improve their services. It had no means of directing capital to where it could be used best to satisfy demand or improve productivity. The only way it had to secure more funding was to obtain it from government, which meant from taxpayers.

Doctors and specialists took to appearing on television to complain that their patients were being denied effective treatment through lack of resources, and demanding more funding for their area of expertise. This was called 'shroud waving', and was a source of embarrassment to successive health ministers and governments.

Another feature of the NHS was that it turned health into a zero-sum game. Money spent on one area of health could not also be spent on another. The funding that might give prematurely born babies a chance to survive might otherwise be used to give elderly people hip operations to restore their mobility. When an item such as health is free to the consumer, the demand can be near infinite. Given a finite budget, however, choices have to be made, and some committee somewhere has to decide whether the premature newborns should have priority over the elderly disabled.

We decided that any reform put forward by the Adam Smith Institute would have to incorporate two features if it were to stand any chance of political acceptability. People had to be reassured that they would receive treatment no matter how poor they were or how sick they were. In practice this meant that any proposed reform should retain the principle of funding health out of taxa-tion and making most of it free at the point of consumption.

The Institute's proposal left the funding virtually unchanged save in one respect. It advocated making private health insurance tax-deductible for the over sixty-fives. It made sense that at a time when private health insurance premiums tend to rise, and people tend to make more use of health care facilities, to lighten the burden on the NHS by giving older people a little help to stay with private health care.

Otherwise we concentrated entirely on the production of health rather than on its finance. We looked for a way in which an internal market could be introduced, similar to that proposed for schools. Just as we were proposing that the money should follow the child to the school chosen by its parents, we were looking to have health resources allocated according to the choices of patients, rather than by the decisions of bureaucrats.

There was a problem with trying to replicate the schools principle in the NHS, though. Most parents can learn about the reputation of a school. Indeed, there is almost a bush telegraph that puts around which schools are good and which ones are bad. Articles appear in papers and magazines, league tables are published, and their reputations spread by word of mouth.

The same is not nearly as true of health care. Many patients might lack the knowledge and expertise to choose between compet-ing treatments, and not know which hospitals were better than others. Patients do tend to trust their doctors, though, and the GPs do have the expertise and judgement to know which the best and worst hospitals are and which specialists have a higher success rate.

This provided a way around the dilemma. Instead of requiring the patients to choose between treatments, we could allow their doctors to do it on their behalf, knowing that in practice there would be consultation between doctor and patient when these decisions were being made.

The ASI published a study entitled *The Health of Nations*, with a passing nod to Adam Smith's famous work. It proposed that GPs should enrol their patients in what we called 'health management units' (HMUs). With them would go the entire annual NHS funding for their patients, weighted by age and category. The HMU doctors would refer their patients for specialist and hospital treatment, paying for such services out of that annual allocation. The HMUs would be large enough to spread the risk.

The ASI did more work on this principle and published *Health Management Units*, giving a more detailed account of how it would work in reality. In retrospect the name was not a good one. Some people confused them with Health Maintenance Organizations because they have similar initials. In fact the HMUs we were proposing were very different from the HMOs which were a feature of some company health schemes in the US. We might have been better to call them by the more familiar name of 'group practices' even though the HMU idea involved rather more than that.

The hospitals and specialist clinics would become free-standing independent organizations, instead of being cogs in the vast NHS machine. Most of them would be on a non-profit basis, but we certainly expected private hospitals and specialists to be taking in NHS patients whose doctor groups referred them there. In effect our proposed reform kept the funding financed by taxpayers, but turned the actual production of health care into the hands of independent, non-state providers.

The idea was that the HMU groups of doctors would seek out the best for their patients, encouraging providers to compete on quality, as well as on price. We expected specializations to develop very rapidly, with hospitals with a good record on particular procedures to attract more and more patients for those procedures. In this way both efficiency and best practice were likely to spread quickly through the health service.

Within the NHS, some hospitals cost much more than others for identical procedures, so we were confident that opening them up to choices would bring savings, enabling more health care to be delivered for any given level of budget.

The reception to such ideas was very encouraging and a prolonged public discussion took place. We recruited doctors, specialists and health economists to participate in conferences and further publications on the subject. It was a very exciting time because everyone knew that NHS reform was on the cards, and many ideas and groups were competing to help shape part of those reforms.

Some groups were backing a form of health insurance. Others wanted American-style Health Maintenance Organizations to be the order of the day. Still others were putting forward variants of the routing-finance-through-the-doctors proposal. The Adam Smith Institute was in the thick of these discussions and devoted a major part of its time and intellectual energy to them.

A Cabinet committee was formed to undertake a review of the various proposals and settle on options that could become government policy. It was an exhilarating period, with ideas from many sources being proposed and reviewed at a fast pace. Some were dismissed on cost grounds; others were thought politically damaging. Word filtered out of its deliberations, and we made sure that its members were fully informed on our proposals. No less important was our need to know what stage its discussions had reached so we could insert policy proposals and ideas at the right time. We met regularly with members of the No. 10 Policy Unit to keep ourselves up to speed on its progress.

The government eventually opted for a purchaser-provider split along the lines that many of those contributing to the debate had urged. The main providers were to be called NHS Trusts, each to be based around a large hospital or a group of smaller ones. The main purchasers were to be District Health Authorities, along with a smaller number of GPs who might chose to become fund-holders.

It was by no means what we had been advocating, although the NHS trusts did indeed break up the monolithic nature of the NHS into smaller units which would vie for the attention of the fund-holders. The District Health Authorities were not the HMUs we had wanted, and seemed to us to be larger and more bureaucratic than was necessary or desirable. The GP fund-holders were, however, quite close to our model, and we were pleased to see that system being given a chance to show how it might work.

We were pleased, too, that private health insurance for the elderly was made tax-deductible. It was a small point, but could relieve some of the pressure on NHS resources.

In the event the GP fund-holders proved very successful. They turned out to be very innovative in seeking out the best treatment for their patients, and introduced many useful health care reforms. It was they who pioneered on-site clinics for their patients to have minor operations on the same premises as the GPs. It was they who led the drive for more same-day surgery so that patients could get home to their families without a stay in hospital. Dr Michael Goldsmith, who had contributed ideas to some of our publications on the subject, was one of the first wave of GP fund-holders.

They were not only successful, but expanded in numbers. Patients of GP fund-holders were being treated more quickly, with higher quality care, and with better results. The policy was working just as had been predicted.

It was somewhat depressing when a Labour government was returned, that its early decisions included ending the GP fund-holders and the tax relief for the elderly. These decisions were taken by Frank Dobson, a minister committed to a socialized health service. He could have taken the view that fund-holding GPs securing better services for their patients would set an example, encourage others to follow suit and generally lift the entire quality of health care. Instead he seems to have thought it more important to have everyone receiving the same treatment, even if it were an inferior one. Fortunately he was not allowed to abolish private health care.

In retrospect we learned that giving health and education to the left was the price Tony Blair paid for acquiescence by the unions and those on the left in the New Labour project. But even he despaired when the internal market had gone – and subsequently tried to recreate it. By then a decade had been wasted.

The final irony is that the NHS fared no better than did schools under the Labour government. Vast sums of money were allocated to both, but brought nothing even approaching a commensurate improvement in quality. This is because the command and control system is itself faulty, and far inferior at delivering quality than one which directs resources towards consumer choices.

Fortunately, in both education and health, more choice is being introduced. In the health service the fund-holding doctors look set to flourish again, in much greater numbers. When that happens I have no doubt at all that standards will rise along with patient satisfaction, just as the ASI said it would in its original report on the subject.

17

RAILWAYS

Most of the Adam Smith Institute's output on the subject of rail travel was the product of one person. Kenneth Irvine is probably one of those who shared the ambition of most small boys to become an engine driver, but in Kenny's case he never quite got over it. We knew him when he was at university in Scotland and later when he worked in the gas industry and for British Rail. He was quite a regular at ASI events, and was throughout that time a railway enthusiast. Eventually he got to play with the biggest train set in Britain.

Kenny was very sad at the way in which the nationalized railway service in Britain, then known as British Rail, had gradually run into the ground. The service was under-capitalized, as many public services tend to be. It was out of date, using shabby rolling stock that in some cases dated from the 1930s. It had not modernized and its working practices were neither efficient nor cost-effective. Its stations managed to combine being under-staffed with being over-manned, and often seemed full of railway staff whose job was difficult to determine.

There was little customer service, either. Remembering his

time working for British Rail he told us how passengers who complained would receive a £20 voucher by way of apology. If they still complained they would be sent another one, but with no remedial action taken to stop the cause of the complaints.

Timetables should have been filed under the fiction shelves of libraries, for trains were notoriously late or even cancelled. Each day brought a roster of cancellations that made the lives of commuters miserable.

British tourists who travelled to France, Germany or Switzerland marvelled at the sleek modern trains they saw, the high speeds they achieved and the standards of comfort. They watched in awe as their TV sets showed footage of Bullet trains in Japan and TGF trains whizzing across France.

The UK privatized the easy ones first. As the government learned how to do it and acquired new skills and confidence, they gradually took on harder and harder tasks. Water was privatized, then electricity, despite a literature that said this was impossible because of 'natural monopolies'. There was a general feeling that the railways could not forever be deprived of the benefits of private investment, competition and consumer choices.

Kenny Irvine had worked out how it might be done. He had studied the privatization of gas, electricity and water. In each of those the infrastructure was separate from the producers, so that several different producers could use the same infrastructure. There were not two sets of electric cables running into every house, but the householder could now choose which producer of electricity was to send power down that one cable.

A similar structure could be used for railways. The infrastructure of track and signals, and perhaps stations could be in separate hands, with companies bidding to run trains through it. Since competing companies probably could not run different trains along the same track each day, they could compete periodically to run services for a set time period.

Kenny knew his stuff. His paper had all the technical details of how it could be done, as well as the arguments as to why it should be done. We published it as *The Right Lines*, and were happy at the reception it received. It was taken seriously from the outset. Dissatisfaction with the train service had reached the levels where everyone knew that something had to be done about it.

The Right Lines stirred up dissent. Everyone, it seemed, had an opinion on railways and different ideas about how British Rail might be privatized. These included extreme ideas such as pulling up the tracks and turning them all into roads! The most bizarre was endorsed at one stage by Sir Ian MacGregor, former head of British Steel and then the National Coal Board. He proposed building roads on top of the existing rail tracks to make a double decker transport system. 'How much steel would that take?' he was asked at one of our seminars. 'Lots!' he replied with a characteristic glint in his eye.

Other ideas floated more seriously included that of restoring the original private railway companies, complete with their distinctive livery. The board of British Rail, meanwhile, lobbied hard to have the railways privatized as a single entity. The CPS advocated return-ing to the old Victorian railway company structure and put out a paper entitled *Reviving the Railways – a Victorian Future?* Most people would prefer to go forward than back, however, and Kenny knew that British Rail was not structured in that way anymore. Intercity services, for example, plied across different regions and infrastructure was decided nationally.

Kenneth Irvine developed his own proposal in more detail, and this became the Adam Smith Institute's paper, *Track to the Future* (an allusion to the movie *Back to the Future*). The ASI held more conferences on the subject and put out more publications, mostly by Kenny himself.

John Major replaced Margaret Thatcher as Prime Minister and rail privatization appeared in his 1992 Conservative manifesto. When the Conservative government was re-elected, despite what the opinion polls had predicted, the project was given the green light. It quickly became evident to us that the Treasury had taken Kenny's proposal on board, and that this was how it was going to be done.

By the time the civil service, the management consultants, the lawyers and the vested interests had been through it, the Bill of 1993 was very much more complex than we had anticipated. It split British Rail into over 100 separate companies. There were twenty-five train operating companies, with most of the network placed under the control of a new company called Railtrack (which was later replaced by Network Rail). We had envisaged it as a public interest monopoly at first, with reform and competition coming in later, but the government had been advised to set it up as a private monopoly.

Discussion still rages about whether and how privatization might have been done better, but as it settled in it became apparent that rail services in Britain were finally becoming updated with better, more modern equipment. The private carriers took more people to more destinations in less time than the old British Rail had done.

Kenny had a further contribution to make. The old British Rail had suffered a complete fiasco with its Advanced Passenger Train (APT). This tilting train had taken years and millions of pounds to develop, but was scrapped after trial runs without ever entering service. The intention was that a train that tilted on bends would enable high speeds to be attained without the long straight tracks needed by such trains as the French TGV. The problem seemed to be that the APT tilted too much for the comfort of its passengers.

Kenny wrote a report we published as *Fast Track Forward*, suggesting that the Italian Pendolino trains were becoming, in effect, a European standard, and should be adopted for high-speed train services in the UK. This is what later happened.

Although we did not pay Kenneth Irvine for the papers the ASI published under his authorship, he had the satisfaction of seeing his ideas bear fruit, and he did not go entirely unrewarded. When the privatization was going through, one of the private operators planning to bid for franchises invited Kenny to join its board, and offered him shares in the company. When they were successful the shares increased considerably in value. His must have been one of the rare cases in which a think tank author made money out of their idea.

18

POLAND AND THE EAST

While the Adam Smith Institute tended to concentrate on economic and social policy within Britain, we supported, insofar as we could, the Western alliance against the Soviet Union. Totalitarian tyranny and state socialism were at the opposite end of the free-market libertarian ideas we advocated.

From time to time we came into contact with peripheral opposition groups behind the iron curtain. There were rather shadowy groups in Britain who sent seemingly innocent tourists to pass on written materials and money to people in Russia, and this occasionally involved people we knew. Peter Young sometimes attended clandestine meetings of dissident groups within the Soviet bloc. He was once arrested as he tried to leave Poland after attending one such meeting of intellectuals opposed to the communist dictatorship.

He wrote a paper for us entitled *Helping Poland*, which we published in 1989 before the fall of the Berlin Wall. It set out the steps Britain might take to assist the development of freedom in its one-time ally. Its cover, which he designed, showed the Polish eagle, significantly with the crown atop its head as it had been in the pre-communist days.

In the Polish elections of June 1989, the independent union-based party Solidarity won 160 out of 161 contestable seats. Although the rigged constitution had guaranteed the communists and their allies 65 per cent of the senate seats, Solidarity had persuaded the communist allies to defect and join with them in a coalition government which now had a small majority over the communists.

In the summer of this uneasy transition, a group of prominent Poles asked the Adam Smith Institute to hold a seminar in Warsaw on how Poland might be transformed from a centrally planned communist economy into a market-based free enterprise one. We accepted, but since times and conditions were uncertain, we invited a TV crew from the Channel 4 *Dispatches* series to accompany us and film the whole thing for subsequent broadcast on UK television.

The Institute assembled a panel of speakers to hold a two-day seminar in October 1989 on how the various aspects of the transition might be handled. We were met at Warsaw airport by guards carrying machine guns, which the *Dispatches* team duly filmed. I expressed surprise that they had been given permission to do this and was told, 'Oh, we didn't ask.'

Our star speaker was Oliver Letwin, who had taken part personally in some of the UK's privatizations in his work with N. M. Rothschild, and went on to become a leading frontbench MP. (He was the son of Professor William Letwin, one of our original panel of supporting scholars.) He was articulate, confident and persuasive, helping to convince the Poles that the problems could be solved one after the other, just as Britain had done.

We discovered to our great pleasure that although Poland had no stock exchange, it did have a 'fishermen's hall' in which people had originally gone to trade fish, and were now dealing in blocks of shares.

The seminar itself was a slightly surreal affair. Poland had for decades been subject to an economy in which even the number of toilet rolls to be produced was decided by a central committee of planners. Their job was to calculate what the demand might be, and then ensure that enough paper was produced, workers hired, the toilet rolls manufactured and distributed to the various places that might need them. It was a momentous task in which, of course, they failed, as did all of the command economies.

Now we had to put across the point that in a market economy different people might want to make those estimates, commit resources to producing toilet rolls and sell them at a profit if they were right.

'But how can you guarantee that enough of them will be produced?'

'You can't, but market economies get it right most of the time, whereas command economies are always characterized by queues and shortages.'

The translators we had engaged had problems with some of the vocabulary. They were not quite sure what words and phrases such as 'under-capitalized' meant. The *Dispatches* team had a great time capturing some of the confusion that the seminar revealed.

The seminar went reasonably well, however, and several of those attending later went on to join Poland's economics ministry and actually implement that country's successful transition to a market economy.

A potentially embarrassing moment came at the final celebration dinner to wrap up the seminar when the restaurant insisted on following the official rules (which few other people did) and only take payment in Polish zlotys. We didn't have any and no one took credit cards at that stage. Fortunately the difficulty was easily resolved when we went out to the street and called out 'dollars'. A small crowd gathered and eagerly helped us out, and we ended up with far more than we needed.

That visit to Poland in October 1989 convinced me that communism was dead in the water, and that the Cold War had been won.

The *Dispatches* programme duly appeared as a thirty-minute documentary on Channel 4 under the title 'Privatizing Poland'. It was actually quite funny in the way it conveyed the earnestness of the effort and the sometimes not-quite-meeting-of-the-minds. It presented a bizarre, slightly surreal picture, with misunderstanding, uncertainty and false steps, but it was a fair representation of what things were actually like during the fall of the Soviet system and the rise of a market economy to replace it. By the time 'Privatizing Poland' was repeated on Channel 4, the world had changed. The velvet revolution had swept through Czechoslovakia and the Berlin Wall had opened. It was one of the most exciting times I remember. The world we had known and grown up in was changing every day – and very much for the better. The socialist system which many on the left had wanted to foist upon Britain collapsed to rubble, just as the wall itself was taken apart in pieces.

In a few short weeks Europe had become twice as big as we all thought it had been. The ASI published *Wider Still and Wider*, urging the admission to the EU of the newly freed states, and the admission into a wider union of the Eastern, Baltic and Balkan states.

Invitations began coming in from some of those states inviting ASI speakers to address groups of the civil servants or to speak at their seminars and conferences. We were happy to do so, and it was fascinating to watch the transition taking place in many of them. In quick succession I attended meetings or conferences in Hungary, Czechoslovakia (as it was then), Poland again, Latvia, Lithuania and Estonia, while Eamonn and Peter Young did many of the others.

When Eamonn visited Estonia, every food outlet had only the same things: sausages in a thin gravy followed by jelly. His host had to knock on the door to command attention, and the staff would usually come down to say they were full. When they did eventually talk their way into one, they were the only customers. They were given menus, but the host asked which dishes were actually on that night, and was told it was sausages and jelly.

On the last night of his visit they had a big dinner on the top floor of a hotel. The lift did not stop at two floors because these held what had been the KGB listening rooms. They are now a museum. As they looked out at the Baltic, one of the hosts was reduced to tears. For nearly all his life, he had not been allowed to go near the sea, which was barred off from the public by barbed wire and military posts, just in case anyone thought of paddling over to the West. The menus came round and the host asked what was on. 'Why, everything,' said the waiter. Everyone dissolved in laughter. Such a risqué remark would once have landed him in deep trouble. They ate sausages and jelly, but Eamonn reported that the frisson of freedom in the room made them taste sweeter.

Since I was also doing speaking tours of the United States, Canada, Australia and Western Europe, it was quite a packed schedule. This period of frantic international activity coincided with a very busy period for policy-related activity in Britain, yet the Adam Smith Institute still consisted of its two directors, two or three students and Jeanne Hill, a part-time member of the team. We were still trying to do a great deal on very limited resources.

It was not the details of the UK experience of market reforms that the Eastern countries wanted as much as the general principles that governed those reforms. Several times we met the concern that they wanted to be sure they had it right before they began. In the sale of state assets, for example, how could they be sure they had set the price right? We tried to encourage them by telling them it was a learning experience like swimming, in which you became better by doing it. There was no 'right' price, only different ways of trying to secure the best price you could, while giving the enterprise a reasonable chance of succeeding on its own in the private sector.

In many cases the state assets were literally worthless, and had to be simply abandoned despite all the expense it had taken to create them. It was easier in some cases to build up new industries completely from scratch than to try to modernize and make efficient the lumbering giants that had characterized their central command economies.

We once met the response from a senior civil servant, 'This will be very interesting. We have never run a market economy before.' We explained that market economies tended to work better when nobody was trying to run them.

Fortunately there was no shortage of enterprise, particularly among young people. Those whose only chance of advancement before had been through the Communist Party and its state administration now stepped forward eagerly into the vacant spaces created by the collapse of the state economies. In only a few years it became evident that the transition to market economies with significant economic growth was being successfully achieved.

The fall of the Soviet empire and the emergence of Eastern Europe into freedom had a profound psychological effect in Britain. It was no longer possible for people on the left to suppose that history was on their side, that Britain might become a socialist state more similar to what had been Eastern, rather than Western, Europe, or that 'scientific' socialism would one day rule mankind.

It had been almost a mantra among the left's intelligentsia that the outcome of the great struggle between democratic capitalism and state socialism would be a kind of half-way house. The reality was that one side had won, and it set the seal on the market revival of Britain in the 1980s. Free enterprise had won out in practice, and free peoples, when given a say in the matter, had chosen it. We knew it was an event that closed an era.

For the first time since the Adam Smith Institute had been set up in 1977 we now felt safe enough to put a brass plate up outside our door telling people who we were. This is something we would never have done in earlier years when times were more controversial.

19

THE CITIZEN'S CHARTER

As the privatization programme was running its course into the late 1980s, we began asking some serious questions of the services that remained in the public sector. If goods bought from the private sector were unsatisfactory, people could normally expect a refund. We asked why this did not happen in the public sector. If the pullover I bought from Marks & Spencer was in any way defective, I could expect to receive my money back when I returned it. Why did this not happen if the health treatment or the education I had paid for in taxation turned out to be no good?

The question was rhetorical. It did not happen in the public sector because public services had little pressure on them to behave in that way. Private firms offered refunds to secure good public relations. They wanted satisfied customers who would come back and pass on the good word to their friends. Public services did not need to attract people; they had their money in taxation and did not have the bottom-line incentive to encourage the people they served to come back; those people rarely had any choice in the matter.

The word 'empowerment' was in the air, and was generally taken to mean the process by which individuals, groups and communities can play a part in shaping their circumstances, instead of having those circumstances largely come about in ways that are beyond their control. Sociological studies talked of giving people 'voice' so that they could participate in the decision-making process.

The Adam Smith Institute was somewhat unimpressed by this approach. We had seen that consultative committees rarely attracted ordinary or representative people into their ranks, but tended to attract activists instead. Furthermore, they often grew comfortable alongside the industry or service whose output they were supposed to be helping to regulate and could be in effect 'captured' by the producers. Given the classic choice between 'voice' and 'exit', exit worked and voice did not. If you could take your custom elsewhere, the producers would compete to keep you happy.

Our approach derived from our insistence that citizens were not merely participants in government through the ballot box; they were also consumers of its services. We advocated that people should, wherever possible, be given consumers' rights in addition to their citizens' right. The Institute published a report entitled *Empowerment*, which said that people who had paid for public services through their taxes were entitled to receive decent services in return.

If they failed to receive services of reasonable quality, something should happen. There should, we said, be some form of redress. It might be a refund of some of the money they spent as taxpayers on that service or it might in extreme cases be the right to secure that service in the private sector instead, and have the state foot the bill.

As to what counted as 'reasonable' services, we were advocating a revolution in public sector thinking. We wanted them to specify what it was they were trying to provide and to give redress if they failed to deliver that. Each public service would have to set out its aims so that the public would know what they were entitled to expect. It was revolutionary because the previous thinking had been that public services did what they could, which was nowhere spelled out in detail, and the public had no option but to accept whatever was produced.

We said explicitly that there were two signatories to the social contract and two sets of obligations. Citizens had to pay their taxes and the state had to deliver something worthwhile in return. We wanted citizens to be more than helpless recipients of whatever government provided. We wanted them to look government in the eye and understand the obligations due by both sides.

As the ASI expounded this position in seminars, conference speeches and publications, it took some criticism from people who thought it demeaned participation in the political process and reduced it almost to a market transaction. We were happy that giving people the right to quality public services with some kind of redress if they fell short could only improve the services.

John Major, who had recently succeeded Margaret Thatcher as Prime Minister was happy to take up the cause of the ordinary person, and announced his intention to establish a *Citizen's Charter* to spell out some of the rights that people should be able to exercise against the various public services. There was some quibbling about the name by people who thought there were no citizens in Britain, only 'subjects'. But he explained that he meant anyone who lived and worked in Britain.

An advisory panel was set up under Francis Maude to launch the process and I was invited to serve as a member of it. We met regularly in the Cabinet Office under the chairmanship of Sir James Blyth (later Lord Blyth), the chairman of Boots the chemist, and with several prominent people from business and service organizations.

Sir James insisted from the outset that the members of the Prime Minister's panel should be paid, and set the level at £10,000 per year for a part-time commitment of a notional half a day a week. I was glad that someone valued my time at a rate of £100,000 per year! I served on this panel from 1991–1995. Sir James humorously cast me in the role of 'theologian', tasked to ensure that the charter itself, together with the various charters produced to cover each service, conformed to sound principles that would enshrine accountability and empower those who received the service.

It was a huge undertaking and we had a high-powered civil service team headed by Brian Hilton to help us to deliver it. In the initial stages the Adam Smith Institute kept up its own programme of meetings and publications on the subject to make the case in public for a charter that had real teeth to it.

The charter panel decided on set-up to hold on tight to six principles and to test whatever we did against them. First there was the aim of improving the quality of public services. Second came the introduction of choice wherever possible. Third, standards should be set so people would know what to expect. The fourth test was that of increasing value for taxpayers' money. The fifth rule required accountability, both for organizations and the individuals who staffed them. The sixth requirement was for transparency, so that people should know the procedures and how complaints would be dealt with in a fair manner.

It was quite a tall order, to put it mildly. After generations of public service in which departments had followed their own rules, sometimes opaque and arcane, we were now asking them to do something new. We wanted them to say publicly what it was they were trying to deliver and what quality of output they could promise to aim at. And it had to be a level that could improve. We wanted them to say how they could introduce more choices for the recipients and better value for taxpayers. We wanted them to make their procedures and ways of handling grievances completely open.

Sir James introduced a very important principle: the charters for each department or service could not be imposed from above as some diktat of central government. Each one had to come from the services themselves. In Sir James's words, they had to 'own' their own charters.

In practice this meant that charter packs were sent out explaining the principles behind the charter and how it would work, and setting out what a typical 'model' charter might look like. Each service or department would then work on putting together their own draft version of their charter. This could take several months. The next stage was a series of discussions between the civil servants and advisers on the Citizen's Charter team and the services and departments. The aim was to knock each draft charter into an acceptable shape.

Some of the first drafts produced overwhelmingly represented the interest and perspective of the producers. 'It is the duty of every citizen to obey the law and to report their friends and neighbours who break it' was not a good first line in an early draft of a police charter. And the Lord Chancellor's Department seemed to think they were there to service lawyers rather than members of the public. While these incidents gave us much merriment, they did indicate the magnitude of the change in thinking that had to take place.

Gradually the individual charters took shape. There was quite an amount of hard bargaining to secure improved standards. We asked questions such as 'How long will people have to wait before their telephone call is answered?' and 'If they complain, how long before they receive a reply?' A good private business takes an interest in these things because they affect its reputation and how people perceive it. The public sector had never had to do it before.

The charter team had meetings with individual ministers and their civil servants to go over the details of their proposed charters. The Prime Minister took a keen interest in the charter and had discussions with us himself. It was, after all, a distinctive project that no previous PM had undertaken. It was an attempt to tap into the ethos of service represented in the public sector and to have it behave as the private sector behaved for commercial advantage.

Sir James was suitably scornful of departments which sounded out their public in surveys to ascertain what they wanted, and then asked 'producer-oriented' questions. 'How many times a day should trains be cleaned,' was, he said, typical of that. The public neither knew nor cared how many times; they just wanted clean trains.

I was constantly pressing for some redress to be incorporated into charters. If the service failed to deliver, what would happen? Would people be compensated in some way? If their train were cancelled, would they receive any money back? I was quite hawkish in trying to gain acceptance for this principle, though I was not always successful because of the constraints on the public purse.

The Schools Charter disappointed me greatly. It did not promise to deliver anything except information. Every parent will be told this; every school will publish that; everyone would be entitled to know whatever. I told them they should be promising to educate children, not to inform parents.

If children cannot read and write and add up to an acceptable standard by a certain age, I took this as a sign that the state education system had failed them, and I wanted some redress to kick in. I suggested in such cases the state might provide private remedial tutors to bring them up to scratch or perhaps the right to send their child to a private school that could do it, with the state paying their child's annual education allocation to that school on their behalf.

It was to no avail. Perhaps the Education Department feared the numbers that might take advantage of such a clause. Nothing except information was to be promised by the charter, and if the child received no education worthy of the name and acquired no abilities or qualifications to speak of, nothing would happen.

We enjoyed more success elsewhere and gradually established in most services the notion that a certain measurable standard of delivery should be attempted, with mechanisms to kick in whenever they fell short of that. It need not be money; in many cases people just wanted to be treated with some respect and dignity, and a simple apology would satisfy them. 'Yes, we fell short of providing a decent service on this occasion, and we are very sorry and will try to avoid such failures in future.'

In some cases compensation was called for, however. We managed to establish the principle with rail travel that the service did have an obligation; it could not simply take your money and then fail to deliver. We managed to integrate targets for liability and punctuality with refunds whenever actual performance fell significantly short of these targets. The aim was to build in a strong incentive for management to avoid having late or cancelled trains.

There were several meetings with Cabinet. These usually took place in the Cabinet room with a selection of Cabinet ministers whose charters were up for consideration. They would sit on one side of the table with the Prime Minister in the middle and the charter team facing them across the table. Civil servants for both sides would sit behind. The talk was usually very frank and refreshingly free of waffle and jargon. We would ask for targets to be toughened, and they would tell us straight out what was and was not possible.

The time was approaching when the Charter would come into operation. There would not be a single D-Day, since not all of the individual charters would be completed at the same time. It would be more of a rolling programme to bring them out in quick succession. This was also a good way of gaining more coverage in the media for each individual one.

John Major called a special Cabinet meeting in Downing Street to go over the whole programme. Cabinet members and the charter advisers were seated around the outside of a huge hollow oval with the PM at one end. Behind them were rows of their civil servants. As we sat chatting, waiting for it to start, officials told us that the PM had decided this would be a 'shirt-sleeve' meeting, with TV cameras allowed in to take five minutes worth of recording, but without sound.

I suppose the aim was to make it look business-like. I usually wore short sleeve shirts with a bow tie under lightweight Savile Row suits as a way of keeping cool in stuffy meetings, and I did note that when the jackets duly came off as suggested, I was the only person in the room showing rather hairy arms. I also noted that Michael Heseltine, sitting next to me, did not remove his jacket when the others did.

One by one the charters rolled out. Most were greeted by a degree of approval from the media, though a few raised eyebrows at how little of the output of some departments could actually be promised once it had to be measured.

The Department of Transport did not cover themselves with glory when their charter was unveiled, though it seemed quite reasonable in many places. During its preparation they said their surveys indicated that people would be satisfied with no more than ten minutes between Underground trains in London, but since they were not able to achieve that, they had settled for a maximum fifteen minutes. Sir James interjected to ask the minister, 'You mean you commissioned expensive market research in order to ignore its findings?'

The problem with their charter launch concerned traffic cones. These were put out to close off lanes during road works and quite often left unnecessarily in place when the road was not being worked upon, simply for the convenience of the crews despite the massive inconvenience to road users. The department announced that motorists would be able to report such cones in order that action could be taken.

The press dubbed this the 'cones hot-line', but it was a PR disaster when it was discovered that the number simply connected to the general department switchboard, with a recording machine at evenings and weekends, when it would be used most. Some in the press used the fiasco to claim the whole charter operation was no more than a PR exercise empty of meaningful content.

It would not have cost the department much to hire a couple of interns to answer a dedicated phone-line and make sympathetic noises to motorists as they took down details to report to the authorities.

The charter was certainly not devoid of meaningful content. On the contrary it brought about a revolution in public service thinking, a revolution which recognized that they had to produce something measurable and quantifiable, and give the public mechanisms to use whenever it failed to deliver an adequate service. What I hoped it did was give the ordinary citizen a new status and encourage them to demand decent services from government instead of simply accepting with fatalism whatever they were given. Sir James put it pithily, 'We have to turn them into a society of complainers because that way we'll see improvement.'

There was one very useful innovation to come. I never knew who thought of it, but it might have been either the Charter civil service team, or perhaps even Sir James himself: the idea of a Charter Mark. The idea was that public service groups could apply for the Charter Mark of approval. It would indicate the attainment of a degree of quality and give them something to strive for.

Applicants would have to satisfy that they had made significant improvements in each of the six areas we had set out at the beginning. They had to supply evidence, and their application would be investigated to establish they had made quality improvements, introduced more choices, set public standards, given better value for money, while extending accountability and greater transparency.

Each year the Charter Panel would award a fixed number of Charter Marks. Like the 'kite' mark of the British Standards Institution, it would indicate that a quality level had been attained, and would be taken as a sign of excellence. We insisted that every application had to be checked out with a personal visit, so we added field trips to our work to check out that the reality we saw corresponded with the paperwork that had been sent in.

I was hugely impressed by the Kent Fire Brigade. It was so highly disciplined and striving for perfection that it rather resembled an elite military unit, with a similar esprit de corps. They deserved their Charter Mark and won it easily. I was less than impressed by the South London borough whose street cleaning unit I visited. Their paperwork had spoken of 'all graffiti removed within twenty-four hours', yet there was some at the side of their own front door when I visited, plus several decorating the borough's streets. The unit seemed like a very small subset of the borough's operations, and aroused suspicions that their wider operations did not meet acceptable standards. Needless to say, they were not awarded a Charter Mark.

When the first Charter Marks were awarded, there was a big exhibition and day of celebration in the Queen Elizabeth II conference centre in Westminster, with a visit from the Prime Minister and some Cabinet colleagues. Those who had won the award were proudly displaying their efforts in photographs and exhibits. The winners were allowed to display the Charter Mark in their offices and on the stationery and leaflets for three years. After that they had to win it again if they wanted to continue to use it.

Did the Citizen's Charter make a difference? The answer is that it did for a time. It made a remarkable difference to the attitudes and outcomes of the public services. I was surprised and impressed by the way in which the civil servants threw their efforts into making it work. Taxpayers no longer just paid their taxes and grumbled when they received poor service. The exercise raised both expectations and quality.

More to the point, it did exactly what the sociology critics have found most objectionable about the idea. It inserted a degree of consumerism into the relationship between a citizen and the government. The Adam Smith Institute thought this an excellent thing in that consumers seemed to have more rights more easily exercised than did citizens.

At the start we had employed a spelling that put the apostrophe after the 's', making it a charter of citizens. We followed the government's lead, though, when they chose to spell it with the apostrophe before the 's', making it the charter of each individual citizen. In our view it was for citizens and redefined their relationship with government.

Talk of greater participation and involvement was all very well, but we thought it a rosy way of looking at an imagined world in which people behaved very differently than they behaved in the real world. Most people do not want the effort of becoming involved in politics at any level; they prefer to pursue their aspirations in their own way and spend their spare time on the things they enjoy doing.

The Citizen's Charter was real world and embodied real rights. The Labour Party, which had originally tried to dismiss the whole idea, rapidly changed tack and began to produce their own version of it. When Tony Blair became Prime Minister in 1997, the Citizen's Charter was absorbed into a wider project for improving public services. The Charter unit was replaced by a 'Service First' team with a remit of modernizing government. This has since closed, so the Citizen's Charter is no more.

It was perhaps expecting too much to hope that it might last. Public services can be made to copy some of the practices of private businesses, but only for a time. Without the pressures and incentives that lead private firms to behave as they do, the very different pressures that work on the public sector will reassert themselves.

Strong leadership and firm management can change the behaviour of the public services for a time, but once the leaders have moved on and the management falls into easy and familiar routines, the impetus will probably dissipate over time. It was a bold initiative and a worthy effort, but ultimately the only way to make many public services subject to improving pressures might well be to make them competitive, allowing members of the public to seek private alternatives if they wish, and to take their money with them.

20

20-20 VISION

From its early days the Adam Smith Institute has always been interested in the future, and quite ready to project forwards to see how it might turn out. We were very impressed by the Henley Centre's 1984 study, *Full Circle into the Future*. We did our own predictions, and I often made the future the subject of speeches, including one to a Mensa conference in 1984.

Our approach has been a very simple one of trying to pick out which developing trends are likely to prove ephemeral, versus the ones more likely to have a more enduring impact on the way the future unfolds. Even while at the University of St Andrews, Eamonn, his brother Stuart and I had produced a mock-up of the front page of the *Daily Telegraph* with the stories it might be running ten years into the future. Part of this was for humorous effect, but partly it was a wish list of things we would like to happen.

While John Major was Prime Minister we sent him copies of something we called the *Socks Manifesto*, which went through several updates. It was not named after Socks, who was then the White House cat, but because we thought it so radical that it could blow your socks off. It was full of policies we thought could be implemented to modernize and transform Britain and its institutions, and the Prime Minister approved of many of its goals. Sir Clive Sinclair saw a copy and suggested we might publish a piece about Britain's future. He was very supportive of the notion that societies should set themselves adventurous goals.

The result was published by the ASI as *20-20 Vision: Targets for Britain's Future*. It was not a venture into futurology in the way the Henley Centre had done, but represented things that Britain might want to achieve.

> The future is not something that rolls onward independent of the actions of human beings. It is something which can be made, in part, by those human beings.

It looked forward just over a quarter of a century into the future to the place that Britain might want to become by the year 2020. It listed one hundred such targets, the things that the nation might feel were worthy of striving for and attaining, and included areas such as education, health, transport, housing and the environment.

In education, for example, we suggested a possible goal of having all children not only literate by the age of five, but having been exposed to a second language as well. We suggested Britain might seek a future in which 80 per cent of students could achieve a pass mark in the lower school examination, with 70 per cent passing the upper school examination at age eighteen. This could be achieved by means of nursery school vouchers and tax incentives, parental choice between a variety of schools, and an education system tailored to the needs and abilities of each child, rather than seeking to impose a one-size-fits-all approach.

In transport we anticipated that 2020 Britain might no longer wish to tolerate petrol- and diesel-burning engines in its cities, but would seek to foster the spread of electric and possibly fuel cell technology to replace them. This was not to be brought about by government directive, but by judicious use of tax incentives.

We suggested a future for high-speed rail links between cities and to connect airports to cities, but saw private capital playing the major role in such developments. We also suggested that more imaginative use might be made of Britain's network of rivers and canals.

One rather unusual suggestion was that some of the innumerable disused underground tunnels and defunct stations in London could be put to use, either as the basis for fast vehicle lanes across London, or as underground car parks to reduce the on-street parking that closes off so much road space in the capital.

There were radical ideas to reduce crime, including high-technology crime prevention and redesigning streets and housing estates to make opportunistic crime more difficult to commit undetected. It suggested legal changes, too, in court procedures, with the previous criminal record of an accused allowed to be brought before a magistrate or jury.

In housing we suggested greater incentives to bring distressed or damaged land into residential use and matching grants to extend living space within houses, similar to the highly successful ones that had encouraged the provision of bathrooms and indoor lavatories a generation earlier. We also suggested that some of the prime agricultural land near Britain's cities might form the basis of new model villages.

It was probably the section on the economy that saw us at our most radical. We thought Britain in 2020 should have an economy that looked and behaved very differently from that of 1994. We suggested that Britain could aim for a growth rate that doubled living standards every twenty years. This would require historic highs of investment – not achieved by government directives but by incentives.

An independent and private Bank of England would be tasked to deliver low inflation rates, which support investment, and the tax system would be reformed to make capital investment more attractive. One of the targets to be aimed at would be the abolition of Capital Gains and Inheritance taxes. The goal for income tax would be for a top rate of 20 per cent and a basic rate of 10 per cent, with government spending capped at 20 per cent of GDP.

We suggested a special category of 'creative individual' could be created, as in Ireland, with remission from even these low rates. For small businesses there might be a special 'artisan sector', similar to that which had been so successful in Italy, exempting them from many of the burdens faced by larger firms. Amongst our proposed banking reforms was the suggestion that banks might take equity stakes in small local businesses instead of just making loans to them at interest.

It was all heady stuff, and offered the prospect of a vigorous and dynamic economy which would pay its share to government finances at low rates over a very broad base. Economic expansion would make up for the low tax rates which themselves would help trigger it.

As we made clear in the section on 'Society, Work and the Family', investment would also be aided by the establishment of our *Fortune Accounts*, the lifetime personal accounts into which people would save for their future pension needs. Not only would these lower the demands which future retirees would make on the state, they would also constitute a huge investment fund to be assigned by their providers.

The suggestions followed thick and fast, and pervading them all was the idea that these were reasonable and attainable targets for

Britain's future. In a news column the diarist Alan Clarke described the report as 'brimming with optimism' and contrasted it with the sometimes very low-key and often timid goals of national and local governments.

In fact our picture of the future saw a smaller role for government, with individuals in the future making for themselves many of the decisions which government currently made on their behalf. We foresaw a leaner, trimmer government, with the closure of departments such as Agriculture, Employment and Transport, and the merging of the various law officers into the Home Office.

We foresaw much wider use of private contractors to perform public functions, including whole local government areas which might choose not to operate their own in-house services at all, but to bring in outside groups to perform them. We thought Parliament might not only want to scythe through forests of regulations, but to attach 'sunset' dates to much new and existing legislation after which it would expire.

Our section on the environment attracted some attention for the surprising novelty of some of its proposals. We suggested that the country's overall tree cover might be raised from 5 per cent to 65 per cent, pointing out that some of America's New England states, despite being heavily populated and industrialized, had tree cover of 85 per cent. We suggested that farming trees might be more efficient and friendly to the environment than great prairie acres given over to rapeseed or lupins, and requiring vast quantities of both fertilizers and subsidies.

Some of the media were intrigued by our suggestion that we might want to restore traditional species, particularly in remote habitats of the UK. We pointed to wolves, beavers and bears as animals no longer living in Britain that we might wish to restore to remote areas.

A *Guardian* report teased us by suggesting that we were envisaging an ultimate post-Thatcherite Britain full of dark forests in which people would face the extreme survival of the fittest against the savage animals that roamed it. This was not quite what we had in mind.

There was a serious point behind this exercise, and Alan Clarke had hit it spot on. It was about optimism, and the confidence that human ingenuity and technology could help make the future what we wanted it to be. We were deliberately combatting the conservative pessimism of the environmental lobby groups which traded in doom and disaster stories and painted nightmare visions of the future world.

Many of them were fundamental opponents of progress, and disliked the way in which economic expansion brought choices and improved lifestyles to so many. Their mantra was that human beings must learn to live more simply, be satisfied with less and stop trying to achieve economic growth. We set against that an alternative future in which people could use the wealth created by economic expansion to fund new and more attractive ways of living, with more choices instead of fewer and with more possibilities for personal development.

Our future was an open and expanding one, filled with limitless opportunities. As well as suggesting the goals which the nation might wish to attain, we also indicated the means by which they could be brought about. This was not an idealized vision of an impossibly unrealistic future; it bore more of the character of a shopping list of goals and an agenda for action. It could all be done if the nation willed it.

21

MAJOR ASSISTANCE

The relationship between the Adam Smith Institute and John Major's governments was a very good one. This was partly down to the character of the man himself; he was always courteous and ready to listen to new ideas without worrying too much about their pedigree. He also combined intelligence with concern for practicality, which the ASI tried to incorporate into its ideas.

While he was Chief Secretary to the Treasury in 1989 he came to deliver our annual Adam Smith lecture, and gave a fine speech with many references to Adam Smith's writing, and also to the work of the ASI. He had even read our *Omega Report* and his grasp of detail was excellent. Much of the speech concerned how market disciplines might be introduced into areas of government that could not be privatized directly.

By the time John Major became Prime Minister the ASI was now established. In the early days government had not quite known what we were or how to treat us, but now we were a known quantity, part of the public policy scene, and people had a clearer grasp through our media coverage of what we stood for and how we worked. By its nature the ASI will never be part of the 'establishment', but it was by now, we used to say, a national institution. People supposed we were much larger and better funded than we were in reality, but they saw enough of our output to evaluate it on its merits.

We had a very unhelpful start into his premiership when the Prime Minister's press secretary did us a bad turn by telling a press briefing that 'the Adam Smith Institute would not be seen as much in Downing Street now that John Major was Prime Minister'. The press thought it represented the PM's view, but in fact it was simply made up on the spot. His press secretary thought that it was a good way to establish that John Major was not simply a continuation of Margaret Thatcher. Not only was the remark not true at all, it was the reverse of the truth because we were in Downing Street much more than before.

Our visits to Downing Street were a good deal less stressful than our last meeting with Margaret Thatcher had been. It had been a lunch arranged by John Whittingdale, her political secretary, and in addition to the Prime Minister featured Sir Geoffrey Howe and Kenneth Baker. It was a fraught affair because it was towards the end of her premiership, and she was in a defensive mood. Whenever we proposed a new idea, she would demand to know what was wrong with what they had already done and what they were doing.

I was quite surprised, never having before seen her in such a mood. 'What are you going to do to help me win the election?' she demanded. I explained that this was outside our remit; it was not what we did. The people we took along from our side did not enjoy it very much. They included our chairman, Sir Austin Bide, and Mike Fisher, the entrepreneurial son of Antony Fisher and a great supporter of ours.

The Prime Minister seemed in a very combative mood, even

with her own ministers. I suppose this was unsurprising, given the pressures she was then under. As we left No. 10, a very concerned John Whittingdale followed us out full of apologies. As we left Downing Street, Mike Fisher turned to us and remarked, 'That was interesting. If you hold another of these, don't invite me.'

It was just a bad day. Throughout her premiership, we enjoyed good, if formal, relations with Margaret Thatcher, and very good relations with many of her staff and her ministers.

The ASI welcomed John Major's government. We took the view that you are more likely to have a government be receptive to your ideas if you praise it for what it does right than if you are constantly slating it for what you think it is doing wrong. A new government brings new opportunities as new ministers take over from their predecessors and bring with them an enthusiasm and a desire to improve things. Basically new governments are often on the lookout for new ideas and we were happy to oblige.

In 1991, shortly after he became Prime Minister, he accepted our invitation to be guest of honour at the ASI's fifteenth anniversary dinner in the following year. We went to town on it, hiring the Banqueting House in London for a dinner for 200 people. We managed to secure sponsorship from several businesses. British Airways agreed to help us with some free first-class tickets for a handful of our overseas guests, so we invited a few of our friends from other think tanks to join us at our expense. Bob Poole of the Reason Foundation, came over from Los Angeles and was quite dazed when BA upgraded him to Concorde for the final leg of his journey.

When the dinner came in June 1992, the Conservatives had unexpectedly won another term in office the previous month and the PM had enjoyed a personal triumph by pulling it off. His majority was slender, but enough to keep Labour out of power for another five years. Indeed, it was this defeat that led Peter Mandelson to take the party in the direction of New Labour, abandoning the socialism that had been its hallmark.

We had, of course, to involve Scotland Yard at an early stage in the planning. They told us we couldn't advertise the venue in the advance notice, so it was hard to tell people where they should plan to go. We eventually said 'a central London location'. One of our potential guests, a Conservative supporter, actually complained to the police, saying that it would be too easy to track down which central London hotels had booked a big dinner on that particular evening. The police, who at that stage hadn't actually established where we were planning to hold it, called us in concern, but the venue was not in fact a hotel. The panic was over because no potential terrorist would be likely to work it out.

A sad recent event had been the death of F. A. Hayek in March that same year after several years of poor health. We printed an obituary on the back of the menus and dedicated the evening to him as well as to Adam Smith.

We were somewhat peeved when the PM's security detective insisted during the meal on moving the lectern and even the top table so the PM would no longer have his back to the window, but we managed to have it done before the speech. John Major gave an excellent address, paying tribute to Adam Smith at several points, and highlighting the government's next agenda, which he called 'the privatization of choice'.

I thought the little gifts we handed our guests were among the most attractive mementoes we had ever produced. We had commissioned small marble paperweights about 3 inches in diameter by 1 inch high, with a medallion of Adam Smith in silver finish embedded in the top and set in little blue ribbon-lined boxes.

John Major addressed another meeting of the Institute the

following year, speaking at a reception we held at the St James Court Hotel in Westminster in his honour. On that occasion he praised the ASI's work in promoting liberalization and privatization, adding that our role was to prod governments, 'if necessary with a pitchfork', to keep them doing the right things.

Our most dramatic meeting with John Major took the form of a reception at Downing Street in honour of the Adam Smith Institute. We invited as many of our friends, supporters and authors as we were allowed (about eighty), and included ten members of The Next Generation (TNG), the ASI's youth group. For a teenager an embossed invitation to meet the Prime Minister in Downing Street is quite something.

One of those on our guest list was Neil Hamilton, MP, a long-time friend and supporter. The problem was that by the time the reception came to be held, he had failed in a libel action against Mohamed Al-Fayed, the proprietor of Harrods who had claimed that Hamilton took cash payments for political favours. The trial had failed because of testimony by Al-Fayed's paid employees and the dubious tactics of an unscrupulous QC, who was later himself exposed as a habitual drunk and a wife-beater. I knew Neil well enough over the years to regard the charge as ludicrous.

However, Downing Street did not want Neil Hamilton to come to the event, since they did not want any taint from the trial to be associated with the Prime Minister. They asked us to un-invite Neil and his wife, Christine. We more or less told them that was their job, not ours. After many phone calls from No. 10, Neil himself called to say he had decided not to attend.

The media did not know this, however, and we were greeted by the serried ranks of TV crews and flash photographers behind the barriers on the other side of Downing Street. They wanted to film or photograph Neil Hamilton's arrival at a prime ministerial reception. They called out to me as I arrived, 'Dr Pirie, will Mr Hamilton be attending tonight?' The *Evening Standard's* cartoonist, Jak, featured a cartoon of Neil Hamilton attempting to scale the security walls around Downing Street in order to gain entry!

All was as normal inside, however. John Major shook everyone's hand as their arrival was announced, and at one point after the reception had started he posed for photographs with our ten TNG youngsters as well as with me and Eamonn and the ASI team.

Several senior members of the Cabinet attended and as the evening wore on, they increasingly went for discussions with each other in a side room, or took the Prime Minister aside for brief meetings. It was obvious from their expressions that there was some serious trouble-shooting going on. I was not told what it was, but apparently it was some European issue that had become of critical concern. The event went smoothly for us, however.

The young people from the TNG group we had invited were asked back to Downing Street a few weeks later for a 'focus on youth' discussion in which the Conservative government sought the opinions of young people in order to assist it in putting its message across to Britain's young voters.

As 1997 unfolded, however, it was becoming increasingly clear that the Conservative government was not putting across a message that appealed to voters. It was perceived of as past its sell-by date and people were looking for something newer and fresher – and thought Tony Blair's New Labour might be it. Its lead in the polls made it clear that the country was going to give them a chance.

This presented us with a problem, in that we had put out ideas to a largely receptive Conservative government and did not know whether a Labour government would want to listen. Their earlier commitment to reverse all of the measures passed by successive

Conservative governments had been dropped, but no one knew if they were sincere. Some people in the Labour Party hoped that New Labour's moderate stance was merely a ploy to win an election, and that once in power they would pursue red-blooded socialism. Others outside the Labour Party feared that this might be true.

The ASI had specialized in policy research that put forward new options. The idea of simply opposing attempts to reverse the free-market gains did not appeal to us at all. That was the kind of thing that political parties did, not think tanks. On the other hand we knew there would be tribal resistance within the Labour Party to taking ideas from the Adam Smith Institute, especially as we had been so close to John Major's government. We decided that while we would be putting what we hoped were helpful ideas in the direction of the new Labour government, we should redirect much of our activity to reach a wider market than the rather narrow group of decision-makers we had been addressing hitherto.

22

THE MORI POLLS

We were heartened by two things that happened right at the start of the Labour government elected in May 1997. The first was in Tony Blair's 'new dawn' victory speech made outside Downing Street and timed to coincide with the sunrise. It included the sentence, 'We ran for office as New Labour, we will govern as New Labour.' This declared to the country that Labour were now sincere about not seeking to reverse the free-market advances made under the Conservatives.

The second came a few days later when the new Chancellor, Gordon Brown, announced that he was making the Bank of England independent and charging it with the task of keeping inflation within a point above or below 2 per cent. Kenneth Clarke, for the Conservatives, denounced the move, but of course the ASI welcomed it. How could we not? It was a policy initiative that had been the subject of several of our publications and we had campaigned for it for over the course of two decades.

Our approach to the new government was generally optimistic. We praised things we thought they were doing right and did not raise too much noise over things they did that we disapproved of.

They started quite well. It was only later when Gordon Brown asserted his dominance over domestic policy that the old Labour habits of tax and spend reasserted themselves. In the first few months our attitude was one of relief that they were not bringing forward plans to renationalize industries or give back to the unions the powers that had enabled them to bring the country to its knees.

During their first few months in office we were able to give them quite a good score, a stance that did not sit well with some Conservatives who seemed to think our job was to oppose everything Labour did. Some of them seemed to regard us as part of the Conservative Party and thought we should have loyally followed its line. Some even criticized us for welcoming the Bank of England's independence, even though we had proposed this very thing ourselves.

The ASI had always described itself as non-partisan and we were determined to maintain that position. Someone speculated in print that I had secretly joined the Labour Party and been taken into its 'big tent', which was utterly ludicrous considering that we had not allowed our staff even to join the Conservative Party, and were not members of it ourselves. We did not join political parties because it would have compromised our free-market message.

In general we found that the New Labour ministers would accept invitations to speak at our meetings and conferences, but those who revered the old Labour Party would not. Since ministers would turn up surrounded by a twelve-strong posse of civil service minders, special advisers and PR people, we generally felt that they were using us as a spinning platform rather than coming to engage in some actual debate about the merits of different policy options. Peter Mandelson had apparently told them not to attend any parties where they might say something injudicious, so it was not just our events that were affected.

David Blunkett happily accepted our invitations, however. He spoke at one of our TNG meetings and drew a large crowd of our youngsters. He stayed behind afterwards to meet people and chat, and seemed completely at ease. When the time came to give him a token gift by way of thank you, we realized that an Adam Smith tie would not be of great use since he could not see it. Instead we gave him a desk-top bust of Adam Smith and watched his face light up with pleasure as he ran his fingers around it.

David Blunkett was very much an exception and our attention was turning, in any case, to ways of reaching a wider audience.

We had met Robert Worcester, the founder and head of *Market and Opinion Research International*, or MORI as it was generally known. He frequented political circles, and we occasionally encountered him and chatted at receptions. Now we went to him with a proposal. We wanted to commission MORI to investigate the attitudes and aspirations of young people in Britain. ASI's youth group, The Next Generation, gave us a pretty good idea of what sort of questions to ask. Since the ASI was not very rich, we asked if there were ways in which this might be done relatively cheaply.

Bob (as Robert Worcester was usually known) was very interested and suggested ways in which we might obtain statistically valid data from a representative sample nationwide. Gradually, over a series of discussions, the project began to take shape. We were interested in young people in their late teens who would be coming of age at about the turn of the century. Instead of going for the conventional advertising groups of Generation X or Generation Y, we called our sample the Millennial Generation, catching both the interest people have in knowing what young people think and combining it with the increasing anticipation of the coming new millennium.

We wanted to ask them questions that brought out their

attitudes to government and what they might hope to achieve in life. These are difficult things to elicit, but MORI arranged them as a series of choices that their respondents might pick out.

When we saw the raw data after MORI had performed its sampling interviews, we realized we were looking at something remarkable. The coming generation had many attitudes that were noticeably different from those held by previous generations. Some things were traditional, such as hoping that a happy marriage with children might feature in their future lives. But it was the ones that were different that impressed us.

Rather than release the data with an accompanying press release as would have been more normal, we decided to make a book out of it, with MORI providing the data and statistical analysis and with us writing up the significance of it. The book was published as *The Millennial Generation*, co-authored by me and Robert Worcester. It was an attractive-looking production, produced in A4 size with a glossy cover featuring a group of young people of the appropriate age. It had a spine, too, so it could be seen on a bookshelf.

We knew something about the Millennial Generation before we started the survey. These 16–21 year olds had spent most of their teenage years in a revitalized market economy against a backdrop of a rising stock market. They had seen steadily rising GCSE and A-level passes, and a higher proportion of them would go through university or college education than their predecessors.

Their favoured recreation was clubbing and some occasionally used recreational drugs. They were more enthusiastically brand conscious than the previous age group and spent money on cosmetics, personal hygiene and foreign travel. They were also the first internet generation with widespread access to mobile phones.

Market surveys had confirmed the visible and anecdotal evidence on these things, but we wanted to find out some things that didn't show: what they thought about government, society and their own future. In consultation with MORI we decided to follow the main survey by follow-up interviews with just a few of them, and putting unattributed quotations from them scattered through the text as occasional insets.

Both Bob Worcester and I liked the co-authorship, his for the research, mine for the interpretation. His name on it lent authenticity to its findings and we were both pleased to have our names on such a nice-looking production. We both thought it might attract a great deal of attention.

There was little comfort for the Conservative Party in its findings: three out of five of those naming a party expressed support for New Labour, whereas the Tories did not even reach one in five. However, the degree to which life had been depoliticized for young people showed up in the fact that over seven out of ten of them thought that government would make very little or no difference at all to their lives.

Large majorities among young people thought it was up to them rather than the government to gain a job and a home. And although a majority did think it the government's responsibility to provide them with an education and a pension, more than one in three thought it should be up to them to do that.

There was bad news for politicians and journalists. They were the two professions that young people respected least, whereas they did respect doctors, policemen and lawyers. Significantly, respect for the police diminished among the older teenagers in the sample.

They were quite a tolerant crowd, with one in three admitting to the use of illegal drugs. A majority of them supported a ban on

Ecstasy, but not on abortion, cinema and TV sex and violence, tobacco advertising or smoking in public places.

The real surprise came with personal aspirations. The highest single career goal (48 per cent) was that of owning and running their own business. When asked about ambition, 43 per cent listed 'being a millionaire by thirty-five' as a career goal. Only 1 per cent looked to careers in the civil service or local government.

We pored over these figures at the ASI, greatly heartened by what we were seeing. The young people surveyed seemed optimistic, self-confident and ready to make their own way in the world. We thought it boded well for Britain to have such ambition coming of age. These people bore the hallmarks of the up-and-coming entrepreneurs who would create the wealth of the nation's future.

The ASI press release that accompanied the book did not mention the phrase 'Thatcher's Children', but most of the papers did. We gave the media a longer lead time than normal to give them the chance to set up their own interviews with young people. Most of them did.

BBC2's *Newsnight* gave an extended section on the survey, with live interviews with some London youngsters. Most of the papers did the same, with many giving the story a full page. Even the broadsheets gave it a half page, many with inset photos and comments.

The Sun disappointed us, though. They loved the story and did interviews and photo shoots to back it up with two or three pages of coverage. None of this appeared, however, because they had overlooked the deadline for its release and missed it altogether! Nevertheless, the story did receive saturation coverage elsewhere.

More to our point and purpose, it set people thinking about the new generation that was coming of age. Their attitudes and values had been affected by the changes that had been undertaken in Britain and now it was beginning to show. They were more confident and self-reliant than their predecessors, and more convinced that they could personally achieve things.

The fact that they looked less to government to provide for them was a good thing as far as we were concerned, because it was an outlook that fitted naturally with the break-up of the old state monopolies and the introduction of personal choices. They rated education and determination more than background and connections as ingredients of success.

It was an important milestone for us because it confirmed that we could still advance our ideas and our agenda even with a government that did not share our degree of enthusiasm for free markets and individual choices. We could put our ideas across more elliptically and to a much wider audience.

STUDENT LIFE

We decided to follow the success of *The Millennial Generation* by taking an opinion poll snapshot of student life and outlook. We wanted to test how they behaved, how they spent their money and what they thought of other students. We wanted in addition to test what they thought of their education and who should be running it. As with the previous survey, we wanted to know what they thought of government, what they expected from it and what personal qualities they thought most important to achieving success in life.

Again we went to Bob Worcester and MORI to set up the sampling. Bob suggested that we pick a selection of universities that would include most of the different types of institution as well as giving us a good geographical spread. On MORI's advice we settled on ten universities that included big city universities, small campus ones, those in London, Wales and Scotland and one Oxbridge one. MORI had done a panel survey for the Cabinet

Office the previous year and we had access to its published figures for comparisons.

We were under no illusions that the selling point of the survey would be the student lifestyle. We regularly visited universities and numbered many students among our TNG group, and had a fairly good idea about how students lived and chose to spend their time. We knew that most students had a very positive experience of university and that although they might complain regularly about the hardships it involved, very few were ever caught trying to tunnel their way out of university.

What we were interested in were things like whether they thought that education was good value, how much their choice of subjects was influenced by career prospects and whether they thought the government interfered too much. We wanted to know how tolerant they were and how indulgent were their own practices and experiences.

Because of the way MORI conducted the survey we were able to add a new dimension to our breakdown. As well as knowing which factors weighed differently between girls and boys, we could now compare the responses from different universities. We knew this would make the survey of special interest to the local media in the places we had chosen for the sample.

As we had done with the first survey, we examined the raw data obtained by MORI and wrote a commentary on what were its most significant findings. Again it was co-authored by Bob Worcester and me, and presented in a format very similar to *The Millennial Generation*. The glossy cover showed a crowd of Cambridge students dressed up for graduation with the chosen title *The Next Leaders*.

The broad findings reflected to some degree what we had found for the age-group in general in our first survey. Students were reasonably serious about their career choices, but quite ready to enjoy the lifestyle that accompanied the away-from-home experience of university education. Crucially, they were overwhelmingly convinced that their success depended on things within their personal control, rather than on external circumstances determined by society, government or the world economy. Like the Millennial Generation, of which they were part, they were optimistic.

After we had sent out copies with our press release, once again allowing time for the media to prepare their own back-up stories to accompany the survey's findings, we had a very awkward moment when the London *Evening Standard* inadvertently quoted one of the poll's findings. The *Manchester Evening News* called us to say that since the embargo was broken, they wanted to run the story on the afternoon before its release.

We knew what would happen if they did. Given what it showed about Manchester, they would run it as a front-page story and all hell would break loose. The TV news channels would then feel free to cover it, and the main national dailies would scale back their coverage of what would then be seen as 'old' news. We told the Manchester paper that the one figure that had been published did not alter the embargo. They were annoyed at missing a potential scoop, but they kept to the rules.

The next day the story received big coverage in the newspapers, as we knew it would given what it revealed about student life and attitudes. Students turned out on the whole to be quite sympathetic to their university administrations and would prefer them to be more independent from government. This sat well alongside our own agenda which looked to a future in which universities might be independent of the state altogether.

By an overwhelming margin students thought that a university education represented a superbly worthwhile investment for them. This was not altogether surprising, given the higher salaries that graduates could look forward to, but it was good to see it so strongly confirmed. The finding might have given encouragement to those who thought that students might make more contribution towards the cost of their education.

University students tended to be personally very tolerant, neither racist nor homophobic. Most of them had gay or lesbian friends, along with those from ethnic minorities, and most of them were friends with, or knew of, regular users of illegal drugs. An interesting fact that emerged clearly was that students were not very tolerant of intolerance. Not many included any religious fundamentalists among their friends and even fewer admitted that they had any racist friends.

The scores for drug use were highest in Manchester and London, maybe because of the strong clubbing scene in both cities, sometimes linked with drug use. Manchester came top for sex, as it did for drugs. There 40 per cent answered that they had sex at least once a week, against the overall student average of 31 per cent.

The authorities at Manchester were not pleased by our findings and we did receive a couple of irate phone calls. We carefully explained that the press had 'sexed' up the findings and that we had not used the word 'Madchester' in our report (though some of the press had). Considering that central Manchester is said to have the highest concentration in Europe of students attending the various academic institutions there, combined with all that goes on in big cities, we were not surprised by the findings. The university authorities were alarmed in case worried parents started to urge their children to avoid Manchester and its temptations.

When it came to career choices, three in five students singled out 'working with sociable and friendly colleagues' as a key determinant, with just under half pointing to high salary as a motive. This again fitted broadly in with the findings of the Millennial Generation. The students identified the top ingredient for success as determination, just as we had found in our broader survey of the age group. The students placed educational qualifications not far behind.

We guessed that people would be interested to learn how students spent their money and had asked them how much they spent on various items. Two-thirds reported spending more than £10 per week on drinks, with an average spend of £20. Once again Manchester topped the bill with students spending over £25 a week on drink.

Overall the average student spent four times as much on drink as on books, and spent more on entertainment, clothes and personal convenience goods than on books. We pointed out that good university libraries could make it unnecessary to buy more books.

The story was not quite as big as our Millennial Generation had been, but it was still widely covered and provoked a few editorials. What the story did was to put numbers onto a general observation. People were aware from their own or their children's experiences that students generally have a good time at university. They enjoy its social life and most come away with good qualifications that help them into jobs.

That general awareness now had numbers and percentages put on it. We presented a snapshot of how students lived and what some of their attitudes were. It cleared the ground for subsequent reform of higher education. The ASI wanted even more people to have access to this experience, but thought that the expansion could be funded by loans more readily than it could be out of higher taxes.

TURNING OFF GOVERNMENT

Our third joint project with MORI was an investigation into the involvement of young people in the political process. We were interested here in the attitudes of the 15–24 age group and had the advantage that we could also draw on a previous survey that MORI had undertaken. We suspected that the low expectations from government that had emerged so clearly from *The Millennial Generation* and *The Next Leaders* would show itself as a general disengagement from politics by the younger generation.

At the ASI we thought that people were more likely to participate in politics when it made a big difference to their lives. As more and more of life's decisions took place outside of the political process, the incentive to become involved grew weaker. Thus although people in the political and media establishment generally decried and deplored the disengagement of young people from politics, we were by no means censorious. We took it to be a rational response to the fact that politics did not matter as much as it once had. And we thought it a good thing that more decisions were taken by individuals and families instead of being decided by majority vote in elections.

We published the findings in a book entitled *The Big Turn-Off,* once again co-authored by me and Bob Worcester. The findings coincided more or less with our expectations, though there were a few surprises. We found that young people were noticeably less engaged in or interested in politics than their counterparts of thirty years previously.

They were far less likely to vote in local government elections and by a huge margin denied it was the inconvenience of doing so that deterred them. They were dismissive of the various proposals to make it easier to vote. They were not going to vote because they were not interested and they did not think it would make any difference.

Very few of them expressed any community identity at any level, be it to their locality, their country or to Europe. In every case, fewer of them felt loyalty to any of those. A smaller proportion of them claimed any knowledge of local government, Parliament or Europe. When asked about citizenship, most of them thought it was about a way of behaving and having regard for others, rather than of specific duties and involvement.

It must have come as a splash of cold water to the political establishment, to whom interest in politics is a way of life. In interviews we were more sanguine. We said that the political classes enjoyed being in politics and declared it to be everyone's duty, whereas most young people thought of it as slightly strange and preferred to spend their time more profitably on entertainment, enjoyment and hanging out with their friends.

FACING THE FUTURE

We were anxious to test the general mood of the nation as it faced the new millennium and did more work with MORI to test people on what kind of future they thought was coming, in particular on what Britain's role might be.

The ASI published it, again authored jointly by Bob Worcester and me, as *Facing the Future*. This time the poll looked at every age group because we wanted to compare what young people thought with the views of their elders. The result was a curious mixture of optimism and pessimism about what might happen by the middle of the dawning century.

A majority of people thought that Britain would still be an independent nation by 2050, though they also thought it would have less influence on world affairs. Of the minority who had any views at all on the matter, more of them thought Britain would lose its cutting edge in science and technology over the next fifty years, and that over the same period it would lose any leading role in cultural and artistic achievement.

A big majority reckoned that Britain would still be a monarchy by 2050, and two out of three thought that ties with America would grow stronger or remain the same. Only a small minority thought that people in this country would think of themselves as European first and British second.

On scientific progress people were optimistic on two things: the spread of instant free communications and the replacement of fossil fuels by non-polluting energy sources. They were more skeptical about other predictions such as flying cars, a 200-year life span, the restoration of extinct species, discovery of extra-terrestrial life or holidays in space. Most people thought these would not happen in the coming half century.

Most expected that there would be more opportunities for people to live rewarding lives, that living standards would be higher and that another world war would not take place.

The ASI found it particularly interesting that huge numbers of people in Britain expected most people to be paying for private provision of most public services. More than half thought that for health, pensions and welfare provision, most people would be relying on the private sector in fifty years time.

It was quite a mixed picture that emerged overall, but one that left plenty of clear ground for innovative policies to be proposed that went along with the general opinion of what the future might bring. As with the other surveys we did with MORI, it showed people looking to a future that held a diminished role for government.

What we were trying to do with all of these MORI surveys was to wean people from a dependency on government. The Britain we had grown up in had featured an all-embracing welfare state, a huge state housing sector, state-owned and state-run industries and utilities, and mass state provision of standardized services. We were looking to a future with more choice, more variety and more independence for people to undertake more of their own provision. In effect, we were using their own changing thoughts about the future and their relations with government in order to encourage them to accept and welcome the changes that were coming, and that we wanted to help to bring about.

WRONG PUBLIC SERVICES

The fifth and final book I co-authored with Bob Worcester following a MORI survey was *The Wrong Package*. This took a different tack. Our aim here was to show, through polling, that the public services set priorities and an output that in no way corresponded to what the public, their consumers, actually wanted them to do. We wanted to show that the public services exhibited a producer culture instead of the consumer culture that most private sector services strive to inculcate.

Our survey therefore invited respondents to select what they thought should be the priorities of each service, which amounted to saying what they wanted the service to do. They were also invited to pick out what they thought were the lowest priorities, or the things they did *not* particularly want the service do. We concentrated on police, schools and local government, and found a wide divergence between what people actually wanted from them, and what those running the service delivered.

By large majorities the public wanted the police to target criminal gangs, muggings and street crime, to deter crime by their visible presence, and to prevent burglary and recover stolen property. What they least wanted the police to do was to arrest those using force to protect their homes or property. They thought enforcing speed limits on motorists should be a low priority, and lower still came counselling victims of crime and building good relations with ethnic minority communities.

Those low priorities are all fairly easy ones for the police to do, and can be ticked off target sheets and check lists, whereas what the public wanted was for the police to actually cut down crime, which is very much harder to do.

When it came to the schools, the public wanted them to concentrate on basic skills such as reading, writing and comprehension. They wanted children taught in smaller classes, alongside children of similar ability. Their lowest priorities included school uniforms, making passing exams the first priority and raising teachers' pay. The numbers supporting a concentration on basic skills were striking, with 62 per cent in favour and only 1 per cent thinking differently. By a margin of three to one people supported streaming, and did not want brighter children held back by having to be taught alongside those with lower abilities.

In local government services, too, people supported the basics. They wanted crime and vandalism deterred, by CCTV where appropriate. They wanted council estates kept in good repair, with action on graffiti and dog dirt, and they thought councils should be tough in moving on problem families.

They were least concerned to have local government employees trained in racial awareness, or to ensure they enjoyed good pay and working conditions. The public gave both counselling and local library facilities low priorities, too.

What the ASI was attempting to bring out through this survey is that it is perhaps endemic in the public services that they do produce what is easy to produce. With private services people will give their custom to those that meet their needs and priorities, but they do not have this choice in state-funded public services. The incentives are not there, and nor is the information obtained by seeing where people take their custom.

In the absence of choices for the public, the ASI took the view that public services should take care to find what people actually want, and then attempt to deliver it.

We were also aware of the cost factor: the things the public wants might be expensive to achieve, whereas cash-strapped public services might prefer to deliver things that are less costly. Counselling and diversity awareness are relatively easy things to produce, whereas breaking up organized crime is almost certainly harder to do and more demanding of resources.

Overall, the Institute regarded these MORI polls and the reports it issued based on them as a worthwhile exercise and a good way of putting our point across to a wider audience. The press finds that opinion poll results and lists make good copy, and are likely to cover the results. This means that legislators and opinion formers can have brought to their attention public attitudes and priorities they might not otherwise have known about or taken into account, and that, in turn, can have an impact on the legislation they might bring forward.

The only thing that prevented us from doing more of it was the expense. Professional opinion polling is not cheap, valuable though it can be.

23

ONLINE

The Institute tried to be reasonably tech-savvy. We started in 1977 with IBM golf ball and cartridge electric typewriters brought back from the US, used with bulky transformers. Then Mike Fisher of Whale Tankers, the son of Antony Fisher and a keen supporter of the ASI, gave us one of his surplus word processors together with a huge machine which copied and collated and was dubbed 'the beast'.

After the word processor, the ASI graduated to Epson and Kaypro computers, buying several of them in the US and carrying them back as hand baggage on the flights home. We made one big mistake in listening to the advice of one of our young interns. About to buy Apple Mac computers, we were told that PC machines now had Windows which was 'just as good' and much cheaper. It was a mistake we regretted for two years until we finally reverted to plan.

On a day we designated M-day (for Macintosh) we junked the PC machines we had found so clunky and non-user friendly, and replaced them with Apple Macs. Within two hours we were completely fluent with the new systems and have been an all-Apple office ever since.

Part of our strategy of reaching a wider audience led us to set up an ASI website early in 1996. We could never have afforded to do this professionally, and lacked the skills to do it in house, but were fortunate to have as a supporter Mark Griffin whose earlier career had been with Kray super-computers, and who knew what he was doing. He sent us a proposal and entered the figure 'zero' on the cost line as a contribution to the ASI's work. He was just setting up as a website designer, and thought our name was a prestigious national one therefore his involvement with us would be a good loss leader to attract other business. He was someone else that I first became friends with in Mensa.

We were the first UK think tank to go online, and made an occasion of it by inviting Ian Taylor MP, then Technology Minister and an ASI author, to make a short speech at a reception in our offices and to press the key that took us online. Our site was slightly quirky, reflecting something of the ASI's personality. It conveyed a somewhat irreverent attitude with an abundance of information and some humour.

Shortly after this we took a decision to make all of our publications free online from the day of publication. Instead of having to order printed copies and having them posted out, interested parties could now download them as PDFs with no charge at all. It made a fantastic difference to our workload and the general clutter of our office. We no longer mailed out many packets of books every day, surrounded by cardboard boxes of books. The income we had made from their sales was compensated for by the staff time saved.

The other bonus was a vast boost in readership for our publications. Very rapidly we achieved more than ten times the circulation we had enjoyed for printed copies and it soon became much more than that. We had always practised a covert dual pricing policy of charging government and businesses but sending them out free to students. Now they were free to everyone and it was much less trouble. If someone expressed interest in a publication, we simply e-mailed them a link.

Our association with young people through our TNG and our internships meant that we kept reasonably in touch with new technology as it developed. Not only that, but they were quite happy to update our site and revamp our software free of charge as a way of supporting our activities.

Alex Singleton, who had spent a gap year with us before going to the University of St Andrews, suggested we might do a blog, and explained what that was. We decided to go for one linked to our website, and brought in the people behind the Samizdata blog to explain the technology, how it worked and instruct us in some of the protocols. We liked the idea of instant daily communication and thought that if we could make it sufficiently readable it might attract some journalists looking for stories to develop.

None of the other think tanks had a blog, so we were feeling our way without guidance as far as content and style were concerned, and had to learn the ropes very rapidly in the first few days. We quickly worked out that regular posts built regular readership, so we acquired the habit of posting at least a couple of entries timed to be published at 7am every morning. We also put a premium on brevity and tried to have no story that took up more than one screen's length. Ours had to be read without scrolling, which meant a maximum of about 360 words.

After a time we realized that photographs to illustrate a blog story added greatly to its visual appeal and started incorporating them wherever possible. We developed a fairly punchy style, though were careful to avoid the bad manners that seemed so prevalent on the blogosphere. Our approach was to be courteous, even with those we disagreed with.

We rapidly encountered all of the problems that people who run blogs come across. There were people who commented with deliberately provocative and extreme statements to hijack any genuine debate and sidetrack it. Worst of all were the ones we were told were publicly funded blog roaches who preferred to sit at home drawing benefit rather than working and could therefore spend all day at their computers. They had the time to dig up and quote obscure papers published in New Zealand a decade earlier which they said impinged on our stories, and it took more time than we had to track them down and find they did not. Other nuisances included obscure people who used our daily posts in a parasitic way to draw attention every day to their own, hoping the links they posted would attract some of our readers to their own site.

We found ways of dealing with these annoyances as most bloggers do. The most effective thing we did was to post the number of comments at the top of the story under the post's title, rather than at the bottom as we had been doing. When people had read an ASI story, the natural thing had been to click on and view the comments below it, whereas now the natural thing was to go on to read our next story.

We added several details over time to improve the appearance and content of the ASI blog. For a couple of years we often featured technology stories to attract the techno-geeks and for three years we ran a 'joke of the day' in the hope that some of those who looked us up every day for the joke might stay to read some of our content ('those who came to scoff remained to pray,' as Goldsmith put it). Most of the jokes were taken and adapted from other joke sites, though we made some up ourselves. It was certainly useful to have a ready fund of jokes to use at the start of public meetings.

The ASI blog had a deliberately informal air about it. When any new interns joined us we would put up their photo and brief biographical notes about them. When we took our young staff on foreign trips we would get them to blog about their experiences. Sometimes when we did things outside of the Institute's work, like hot air ballooning or taking a helicopter ride over London, we would post photographs on the blog with a story about it.

For several years I ran the blog myself, writing most of the stories and formatting them each day. It was quite time-consuming, and I was greatly relieved when I could pass on the duty and confine myself to writing for it occasionally. The ASI blog built up quite a large readership, easily surpassing the other think tanks. That might have been because we had been at it longer or maybe because we had quite a large foreign readership. Again, it was the name Adam Smith that helped us.

Our young staff kept us abreast of changing technology and the opportunities it presented. We began to post some of our meetings on YouTube, especially the ten-minute speeches which featured at our Next Generation meetings. We always had a strict ten-minute rule at TNG receptions, since people would be standing up, and would soon grow tired and uncomfortable if asked to stand still for longer. We therefore had a stopwatch alarm which we set, very publicly, as the speech started. Most people made sure they stopped before the deadline and the embarrassing alarm. Michael Portillo, who was Secretary for Defence at the time, looked positively startled when the alarm went off and he realized his ten minutes were up.

We would have liked to live-stream some of the TNG speeches so that people outside London or abroad and therefore not at our meetings could follow them live on our website, but we had to reject the idea as being too expensive.

Although some of our staff urged us to start doing podcasts, we rejected this, too. It was not the expense that daunted us in this case, but the time and effort it would have taken. We were not sure how big an audience would want to listen to them or how useful to our cause they would be. We had a very clear perception of our role, and entertainment did not feature very strongly unless it attracted readers and viewers we could then put our message to.

We did go into Facebook very early, setting up groups for the Institute, its Next Generation group and specific meetings people could sign up for. A group was even set up for ASI alumni, since by this time scores of young people had worked with us for short or long periods. As with our blog, our Facebook presence was informal, chatty and irreverent.

We were skeptical about Twitter, unsure if there was any great merit in talking to people in messages limited to 140 characters. We opened an account, however, and used it to feed details of our blog posts onto it. It attracted no great following since it was largely mechanical and therefore rather dull. When one of our youngsters began posting regularly onto it, however, it began to take off, commenting on policies that were being proposed, and giving our take on national or world events. It had a mischievous tone to it that perfectly captured the ASI's attitude.

Whatever other descriptions might have been made of the ASI, 'staid' would never have been one of them. From the very beginning the Institute had a tone that was less than respectful of authority and somewhat capricious in nature. It showed in the titles of our reports, in what we said at meetings and in some of the things we did. Our wholehearted embrace of the new communications technology made it possible for a wider audience to see the sense of fun and mischief that accompanied our activities. We acquired a body of supporters we could never have found any other way, supporters who approved of or who identified with that approach.

24

FAVOURS, TRINKETS AND A STATUE

We knew from the very beginning that there was a market for personal items that allowed people to demonstrate their allegiance to Adam Smith and his ideas; while we were at the University of St Andrews the Political Economy Club had produced club ties bearing the likeness of the great man. They were not very good, being made of polyester, green in colour and with garish yellow likenesses of Adam Smith's head printed in diagonal rows.

The Institute of Economic Affairs asked permission to reproduce them. What was acceptable to impoverished students was not good enough for the IEA's business supporters, so the IEA's director, Ralph Harris, produced woven versions with the same basic design, but in four colours. The profiles of Smith were in a more golden colour, on green ties like the original, but also on blue, red and black. These enjoyed a steady sale, especially to US customers.

At this point Don Lipsett, head of the Philadephia Society and based at Hillsdale College, had received permission to produce his own versions, and was doing quite a good trade in many different designs. George Shultz, President Reagan's Secretary of State, appeared on the cover of *Time* magazine wearing an

Adam Smith tie, and they became more popular still. Arthur Burns, one-time Chairman of the Federal Reserve, also regularly wore one.

We decided to produce our own version, using our logo of Smith and in St Andrews's colours of light blue, dark blue and white. Ours were in silk with the head of Smith in a laurel wreath in white against dark blue with light blue and white stripes, and looked very good indeed. We reproduced the profile of Smith by Xeroxing the Tassie medallion of Smith and hand-drawing the leaves around it before scaling it down. This was our original logo, too. Much could be done by improvisation.

The tie sold well, and soon we faced demands for something ladies might wear, so we produced a silk scarf from the same design and I took the opportunity to have a few self-tie bow ties made at the same time.

We then produced some gilt lapel pins of Smith's head and some silver-look medallions in presentation boxes. We did coffee mugs and ballpoint pens in presentation boxes. Bearing in mind the youth of many of our supporters, we had some baseball caps made in the US and shipped over. People in Britain had seen baseball caps in movies and on TV, but had not started wearing them at that stage.

Just about everything that can be branded was done in an Adam Smith version by the Institute. This included calendars, diaries, notepads and wallets. They were followed by umbrellas and briefcases, and we even had a few wristwatches done with Adam's head on the face of them. We had office clocks made as well.

A firm south of Edinburgh offered to make our own label mead, which is one of those drinks that everyone has heard of, but few have tried. We duly ordered a vat of it and had it bottled as 'Wealth of Nations' mead, with a profile of Adam and the legend 'as strong and as sweet as the free market itself'. The reality was that it tasted somewhat weak and was rather sour. One of our supporters who bought a bottle said it needed whisky added to bring up its alcoholic strength (it was about 12 per cent).

The thought led us to have our own-label whisky produced as well. We located a distiller who would bottle a batch with our labels on. We called this one 'Spirit of the Invisible Hand', and put at the bottom of the label 'You will be led to promote an end which was no part of your intention.' We often handed these out to visiting speakers and never failed to gain a laugh when we read out the message on the label.

Our ASI frisbees were very popular and two large orders sold out almost at once. They bore our logo in blue on white, with the message 'Ideas around the world' circling around it. ASI T-shirts were popular, too. When we did ASI hoodies, I hired a graphics firm to design funky lettering so that the words 'Adam Smith Institute' looked like a graffiti tag someone had painted on a wall, complete with paint dripping down from the letters. The design itself was woven into the front of the hoodies, though, not printed on them. Every purchaser of the hoodie received a signed 'ASBO certificate', authorizing them to engage in anti-socialist behaviour.

We had several different versions of Adam Smith busts. I had met the sculptor Barbara Stride through mutual friends in Mensa. She produced an elegant likeness based on contemporary prints of Smith and the Tassie medallion, and we had it cast in resin to look like bronze. We wanted smaller and lighter versions and tried to have them made overseas at low cost. The ones from Nepal, which Steve Masty had made for a pittance, aroused much merriment because of their bulging eyes, and the ones from the Far East gave him a decidedly oriental look. Eventually we found a UK supplier who could make us good copies. By using a material that shrinks when it dries, a large bust can be scaled down in a few stages to make a small one.

After the fall of the Berlin Wall a story circulated quite widely that one of the factories that had formerly made busts of Lenin had melted them down to make ones of Adam Smith. It was a story that deserved to be true because it reflected how the world had changed, but we were never able to confirm it.

For City supporters who wanted to declare their allegiance we produced braces, as worn by Gordon Gecko in the movie *Wall Street*, but ours were in blue with Smith's likeness and name repeated on them.

Not all of the Adam Smith paraphernalia was successful, however. I had been impressed in the US by letter openers that had a recessed blade and could open an envelope cleanly without damaging its contents. I had a few boxes of them made with our name and logo, and brought them back to mail to some of our subscribers and supporters. We received several puzzled responses from people who had no idea what they were…

THE STATUE

All of the other mementos of Adam Smith were dwarfed by the one Eamonn managed to secure. He was in Edinburgh looking at Adam Smith's grave and he observed to the conservator of monuments in the city, Dorothy Marsh, that the large headstone was not in a very good state, being cracked and stained with age. There was even a buddleia growing out of the top of it. He asked if the Institute could arrange to have it cleaned up. He was told that it was policy to allow historical monuments to age gracefully, rather than to have them looking artificially clean and smart.

Eamonn saw the point of this, but commented that it would disappoint the many Adam Smith fans who went to visit it. The conservator told him she would certainly support some other public memorial to Smith, so Eamonn wrote to Edinburgh City Council to ask if this might be possible. In response, the council arranged a meeting with officials from many departments and possible sites were discussed, most of them out of the way or unsuitable in other ways. Suddenly one pointed out of the window and remarked that since the area in front of City Chambers was being pedestrianized, there would be space there for a statue. This was right outside St Giles Church with a commanding view down Edinburgh's historic Royal Mile, and Eamonn accepted the proposal with alacrity.

So far so good, but this was going to cost a great deal of money. John Blundell of the IEA advised him that the best way was to sell 'shares' of $10,000 each until the full cost of between half a million and a million dollars had been pledged. We fully expected that most of the donors would be American, since Americans revered Adam Smith more than people in Britain, and since they were generally wealthier and more inclined to support financially causes they believed in.

At a meeting of the Mont Pelerin Society Eamonn raised the subject with people who were attending, and found volunteers chipping in straight away. The deal was that these contributors would have their names preserved for posterity on a bronze plate at the back of the statue's plinth, but more important than that, they would have the knowledge that one of Scotland's greatest sons had finally been given a fitting honour in his own country.

The next step was to commission a design. Eamonn went to Sandy Stoddart, Scotland's leading sculptor, already responsible for several public monuments there. Sandy, who was subsequently appointed the Queen's Sculptor in Scotland, accepted straight away and started work on a design. He made a smaller scale first in clay, then converted to plaster and finally to bronze. The finished statue would stand 10 feet high on a 10-foot plinth, making Adam tower 20 feet above the Edinburgh Streets.

The design used such likenesses as were known and incorporated details around it to represent Smith's interests and achievements. Ships and bales denoted the trade which Smith had so fervently endorsed. There was even a beehive, which was a reference to industry in the language of statuary, but also an allusion to Bernard de Mandeville's *Fable of the Bees*, which had intrigued Smith and perhaps influenced his thinking.

Eamonn tried to have the Queen unveil the statue and so fixed an unveiling date when she would be in Edinburgh for the 2008 General Assembly of the Church of Scotland. Buckingham Palace identified 4 July as the most plausible date, but kept putting off a decision and we realized that the chance of actually gaining a commitment from them were slim.

Eventually, just weeks ahead of the date, we were told the Queen could not manage to fit us in. By then guests had been invited, so we went ahead anyway. Vernon Smith, a Nobel prize-winner in economics, had been planning to attend and agreed to perform the unveiling. Since he had already booked his flight from the US, it did not even cost us expenses, and Vernon was actually rather touched and honoured to be asked. Eamonn commented to me that the security involved in a royal presence would have pushed everyone well back and made the whole thing more remote. As it was, the event was a much jollier, less formal, more social occasion.

As it was, when 4 July 2008 came round, a big crowd gathered round, right up to the statue itself. A piper played a musical tribute and Vernon Smith said his words. It was the culmination of two days of celebration and commemoration in Edinburgh for contributors and supporters, including dinners, debates and a tour of Smith's old house on the Canongate, with a breakfast that included Smith's favourite food, strawberries.

As the covers were pulled off the statue someone asked Sandy why he'd made Smith look so severe. Sandy replied to the effect that if you walked up the Royal Mile on a windswept, chill February morning, that was the face you would pull. The council gave us a civic lunch in City Chambers, and as we came out we saw that the first tourist bus had pulled up so that its passengers could dismount and take photographs of the statue. The City government knew a good thing when they saw it.

About a month later some pranksters planted a traffic cone on the statue's head during the night. We took this as a sign that the Scots had taken Smith's statue as their own, since this is what happens regularly to favourite public monuments in Scotland and we published the photo on our website.

The statue generated a huge amount of goodwill around the world. People felt that the founder of modern economics, the one person who probably contributed most to the wealth-creating process, had finally received due recognition not only in his own country, but with a world class monument that would endure to honour his memory.

25

BOGUS JOBS, FLAT TAXES AND BETTER SERVICES

Many people grew uneasy during Gordon Brown's relentless expansion of the public sector. There was a widespread feeling that some authorities, especially local councils, were not spending money wisely or carefully. There seemed to be a proliferation of jobs in which the actual work was ill-defined or even unnecessary. There were no hard statistics to back up this feeling, but there was plenty of anecdotal evidence.

The Institute decided to take a snapshot of the problem, but one it could put some numbers on. It asked Jonathan Woolham, one of its supporters, to look through all the jobs advertised in a single month in *The Guardian* newspaper. *The Guardian* was chosen because it seemed to be the main forum where public sector vacancies were advertised, be they for the BBC, government departments, public bodies such as quangos, or local government authorities. Each Wednesday it published its *Society* supplement with many pages of public sector jobs.

The ASI published Woolham's findings as a briefing paper entitled *Costing Jobs*. It was sub-titled 'A month in the life of the public sector', and it said that to read the pages of the *Society* supplement was to enter the world of 'anti-social behaviour co-ordinators, racial equality officers, social inclusion officers and community liaison officers'. It was like political correctness meeting situations vacant.

Jon counted up a month's total of 2,315 jobs offering a total salary of £63,713,000, which gave an average salary of £27,522 per job, or 10 per cent more than the average wage in Britain at the time. This was without adding on the costs of National Insurance, pensions and other non-salary benefits.

He checked with other months to establish that this was just a typical month and estimated that over a year it corresponded to about 30,095 jobs paying a total salary of £828,269,000. By the time National Insurance, pensions and non-wage costs were added, the bill was well over £1bn a year.

While we might know what walking officers and tobacco control officers were, without going into the question of whether such jobs were necessary, there were some job descriptions that left the reader flummoxed, including that of a 'positive activities co-ordinator'. Jon helpfully listed a few choice ones from each week to give something of the flavour of the pages. He pinpointed a benefits take-up worker, a definitive map review officer, a supporting people team manager, a democratic services officer and a diversity co-ordinator.

His case was that while some of the jobs were no doubt essential to the provision of useful services, there were others that seemed to involve rather reckless and pointless expenditure of public funds to no great effect.

Many newspapers carried reports of the piece, and several wrote editorials of their own to express alarm at the scale of the problem. The *Daily Express* commissioned a feature article from the author himself. It was one of those occasions in which a vague background feeling of disquiet was suddenly given something tangible to focus upon. We received one irate phone call from the husband of a real nappy officer, but were able to quote him the Department of the Environment's conclusion that real nappies made no environmental improvement over disposable ones.

FLAT TAX

When Gordon Brown as Chancellor was piling on his stealth taxes and sending public spending through the roof, we became very concerned at the ASI that there seemed to be a shortage of any alternative vision. The stealth taxes Brown loved to introduce were all exposed as soon as he announced them because analysts had revealed his mendacity and now regularly pored over his fine print before it was dry.

Few people were putting forward plans for a possible future that could see the government proportion of the economy diminished. We could. We looked at the performance of Hong Kong, and some of the ex-communist countries of Eastern and Central Europe, and saw how a simplification of the tax code could increase the yield, while reducing its proportion of the economy. The secret was growth. It was a difficult thing to cut government spending, but easier to grow the economy around it at a rate that made it less significant and less harmful.

The Institute had for years been in the forefront of campaigns to simplify and reduce taxes. Our kind of Chancellor was Nigel Lawson, who made it his policy to reduce taxation and abolish at least one tax in every budget. We had published reports such as *Simpler Taxes* and *Simplifying Taxes*, and had pointed out that the compliance costs of complexity were very high. Not only did people have to employ expensive advisers simply to understand the tax code, it also pushed people to manoeuvre their efforts around the intricacies of the tax code rather than into expansion and wealth creation.

Now we thought it was time to come out with a concrete proposal for just such a simple tax system. Instead of taking the thousands of pages that made up the UK tax code, we wanted something so clear that everyone could understand it, and which might be expressed on something about the size of a postcard. We asked an intern from Oxford, Andrei Grecu, himself originally from Romania, to research flat tax around the world.

The ASI published his 2004 report, *Flat Tax – the British Case* and put the idea firmly into political discussion in Britain. It covered the history of dynamic tax reduction under Coolidge, Kennedy and Reagan in the US, and under Thatcher in the UK, showing how lower taxes rapidly brought in more revenue, saw government's proportion diminish and had the rich paying a higher share of the total.

The key intellectual figure in this was Arthur Laffer, whose famous 'Laffer Curve' showed how lower rates could yield more revenue. Andrei showed that the two main driving forces behind this are firstly that flat tax decreases the incentive for people to practise tax avoidance. Flat tax usually eliminates most of the exemptions that people otherwise seek and by lowering the rate it lowers the perceived need to avoid it. Secondly, and more importantly, flat tax promotes growth by making the rewards of work more worthwhile. At the lower rates people put in more effort, more new businesses are built up and more consumer spending is available to boost the economy when people keep more of what they have earned.

Andrei looked at a hypothetical flat tax in Britain with a single rate of 20 per cent and a generous personal exemption. It was a sensational proposal that would utterly transform Britain's entire tax system and tradition. He dealt with the argument that this would simply favour the high earners by pointing out that in countries which had introduced flat tax it had benefitted those on all income levels. Economic growth improves the standard of living of poorer people, where it matters most and flat tax unleashes economic growth.

The report received very wide coverage and provoked some excitement. Several papers asked us to write feature articles about it, and several economic commentators and analysts wrote pieces of their own in support of the idea. We continued to push the idea and late in the following year (2005) we published a report by Richard Teather, Senior Lecturer in Tax Law at Bournmouth University. We entitled it *A Flat Tax for the UK – a Practical Reality*, and once again saw the proposal widely covered in the media.

Richard's proposal was for a flat rate for income tax of 22 per cent, with all higher and lower rates being abolished, along with most of the exemptions and allowances. Significantly, he incorporated an idea we had been pushing for: doubling the personal allowance. Under his proposal it would be set at £12,000, meaning that people who earned less than that would pay no income tax at all, while all income beyond that level would be taxed at 22 per cent.

The idea behind this was to remove low earners from income tax altogether. The ASI expressed the view that those who earned the bare minimum wage for an average working week, or half the national average wage, should not be paying income tax at all. An allowance of £12,000 would have removed ten million people from the income tax net.

Richard answered the point that revenue would be lost under his proposals by showing that economic growth would soon make up the shortfall, as it had done in the other countries that had brought in flat tax.

A further twist came in the story when George Osborne, then shadow Chancellor under David Cameron's leadership of the

Conservative Party, let it be known in response to our report that he, too, favoured flatter taxes. Without committing to flat tax, he thought taxes should be simpler and flatter. Momentum began to build as the idea was discussed in many articles in newspapers and magazines.

The Treasury, still under Gordon Brown's tenure as Chancellor, tried to squash the idea. They put out a statement against the introduction of a flat tax in Britain, claiming that too much revenue would be lost. A short time afterwards the *Daily Telegraph* used the Freedom of Information Act to obtain the original text of the Treasury's report to the Chancellor. Sensationally it showed that the Chancellor had deleted all favourable comments about flat tax, including one that spoke of the dynamic impact it would have on economic growth. He had censored the Treasury report to make it seem more hostile to the flat tax idea than it actually was.

Michael (now Lord) Forsyth was commissioned to produce a Conservative Party report on tax simplification. When it reported it recommended a flat tax and various simplifications. Although George Osborne attended the press launch, his every word listened to by a large crowd of eager journalists, it was now too close to the election for him to commit to any specific tax changes.

The international financial crisis of 2008–09 caught Britain unprepared, and exposed the degree to which spending and borrowing had spiralled out of control on Gordon Brown's watch. The level of UK indebtedness, combined with necessary spending cuts, made it politically difficult for Britain to pursue a flat tax policy, but the ASI's response was that a pro-growth, low-tax policy is the only way in which the relative scale of that debt can be diminished, and flat tax is one important way of achieving that end.

BETTER EDUCATION

We were still intent on promoting the idea of school choice, even under a Labour government which seemed intent on dismantling the internal markets that had just been started when it took office. The Swedish model was our example, not least because on the centre left there was still a residual affection for 'Socialist Sweden' as it had once been known.

We published *A Class Act* by Stephen Pollard, a leading left-of-centre commentator. We held a seminar on the subject in Portcullis House, with Andrew Adonis, the No. 10 person charged with improving the schools, in attendance. Our aim was to make school choice command, or seem to command, broad cross-spectrum appeal.

It was during this project that Eamonn went with Matthew Young, who had organized the *Better Education* project for us, to meet the top people in the schools department of the Education ministry. They thought they were making good progress until, just as they were leaving, one of them said, 'we are really looking forward to running the diversity agenda'. Although this was one of Tony Blair's then-current buzzwords, it made us appreciate the gap in thinking. No one runs diversity.

We continued to publish our own papers expounding school choice, or 'open access' as we were now calling it. We published the results that it had achieved in both Europe and America. It felt at times as if we were talking to a brick wall. The government was committed to centralism and big spending in education, as if the entire problem with schools and low standards had been lack of resources. The government wanted quality measured entirely by inputs such as amount spent, teachers' pay, class sizes, whereas we wanted it measured by its outputs, meaning whether or not it actually taught the children anything.

As Gordon Brown was testing to destruction the idea that all public services needed for improvement was more money, we noted two good signs. One was that the Blairites in government were beginning to be upset that all of the money thrown at education had made no proportionate improvement and they were looking for other solutions, ones that might actually bring results.

The other was that the Conservative opposition was now increasingly enamoured with the way schooling was done in Sweden following the reforms there. We began to take heart that it might happen.

HOUSE OF COMMONS BREAKFASTS

A significant series that Matthew Young helped us to start were the House of Commons health breakfasts. The breakfasts themselves were probably not all that healthy, but the subject was. We invited in top NHS and private sector players, sometimes 100-plus at a time, to eat with us and talk about the latest proposals to bring private sector involvement into health care.

Tim Evans, as a director of the Independent Healthcare Association, was a leading player in this effort. He tirelessly made the case that private sector facilities could be used by NHS patients to speed up treatment times and reduce waiting lists, at a cost of no more than the NHS itself was already paying to use its own overloaded facilities.

The breakfast meetings looked at ways in which the private health care sector could work in partnership with the NHS to improve outcomes. The case was so overwhelming that only an ideological opposition to anything which was not state health care could really oppose it.

There was a breakthrough when Tony Blair, desperate to gain improvements that the extra cash had failed to deliver, instructed

Alan Milburn, his Health Minister, to sign a 'concordat' with the private providers, allowing the NHS to outsource treatment. The previous winter's flu epidemic and tales of patients on trolleys in corridors prompted the decision.

A series of such initiatives seemed to us to be a rational strategy, given the government's general reluctance to embrace market reforms. It received no major coverage, but officials from national and local government attended project meetings like these and went away with initiatives to consider. And it did keep the ideas bubbling along while the Conservatives went about the process of formulating in opposition the policies they planned to execute if they gained power.

26

ROAD PRICING AND LAND ECONOMY

Since the Adam Smith Institute made a point of bringing forward market-oriented solutions to policy problems, urban transport featured many times on its agenda. The problem is one of overcrowding, of traffic jams in cities that were never designed for the volume of motorized traffic. The solution of compulsion never appealed to a libertarian think tank such as the ASI. Banning cars from city streets limits choices, so we published alternative solutions.

The Institute has repeatedly made the case for road pricing, for some mechanism that charges motorists for their use of the road. Starting in 1982 with *Private Road Ahead* and *Roads and the Private Sector*, the ASI had suggested that modern technology enables road users to pay for their road use with charges that vary according to the time of day. Those who did not need to use their vehicles during congested rush hours would have a financial incentive to use the road at less busy times. And particularly busy routes would carry higher charges, providing an incentive for people to use alternative routes if they could.

The ASI coupled this proposal, made in a series of its reports, with suggestions that Britain might facilitate the use of 'paratransit' vehicles. These operate in many of the world's cities, and are basically minibus-type vehicles that pick up passengers like taxis, and drop them off along fixed routes but without using bus-stops.

Our 1980 proposal in *The Paratransit Light Vehicle* was for luxury light buses that would pick commuters up at their homes and take them to their place of work, repeating the run in the evening. We envisaged something that might tempt commuters out of their cars by suggesting that passengers would reserve their airline-type seats by monthly contract, and that newspapers and hot drinks would be available on board. During the hours in between the outward and homeward runs, the vehicles could pick up passengers along designated city routes.

We partly based this proposal on the evidence that business commuters would travel by train, or in a chauffeur-driven car, or would drive themselves. In some cities, especially on the Continent, they would use trams. They regarded buses as too down-market and inconvenient, however, and without enough personal space. Our luxury light buses were an attempt to devise a transport system they would accept. The door-to-door convenience, plus their own (reclining) reserved seat with on-board facilities were an attempt to redefine the product.

The one thing that would facilitate this would be to make the monthly contract a tax-deductible business expense. The Treasury would not hear of it. They did not allow the cost of travelling to and from work to be deducted from taxable income, however it might be done – not for cars, not for trains or buses and not for paratransit light vehicles. Not for the first time we encountered a Treasury mindset that saw only a static economy with a bottom line of potentially lost revenue and no costing of the gains that might be achieved.

We pointed out that each twelve-seater paratransit vehicle taking business people to work could take eleven cars off the morning and evening roads. It could take eleven fossil-fuel-burning engines out of the atmosphere. It would create a job for each driver, of whom there might be thousands. No dice. One of our supporters actually began operating a small fleet of paratransit vehicles under the AMOS moniker, but without that tax deductibility there was insufficient advantage.

Progress was made with road pricing, and we kept returning to the subject as more cities in the world began using versions of it, and as advances in communications and monitoring technology made it easier to automate. A few toll roads were eventually built, although this was more basic and expensive than the technology we were advocating.

During the Blair years Matthew Young, who had the knack of being able to organize big events for us, put together a huge ASI project on road pricing in cities. We raised the money to pay consultants £100,000 to report on it and design a scheme for London. At the end of this exercise, London's Mayor, Ken Livingstone came to a project conference and said he was not just willing but determined to do it. And he did.

Congestion charging in London finally established the principle that traffic flows could be controlled to some extent by charging drivers for their use of the roads during set hours, and persuading some to re-time their journeys outside of those hours. It also established that this could generate a revenue stream that could have drivers rather than general taxpayers pay for road improvements. Again, it was not the system the ASI had advocated, but it did show how road use could be paid for by drivers and how modern technology could set up ways of doing it that did not themselves slow down traffic.

DEVELOPMENT AND PLANNING

One of the clearest issues that separated the Adam Smith Institute from traditional Conservative thinking was on the issue of planning controls and development. Many Tory voters who could afford to live in pleasant countryside opposed any kind of development at all. They had their nice surroundings and pleasant views and did not want to see any more building take place. It was not so much NIMBYs (not in my back yard), but BANANAs (build absolutely nothing anywhere near anyone). Tory MPs from the counties tended to represent these attitudes.

At the ASI, on the other hand, we saw an increasing population, an older one, one that chose more and more to live alone. They faced a planning policy which made it very difficult to gain planning permission for new housing. The green belts around cities were mostly off limits, which meant new housing had to be further out, adding even more to traffic congestion for commuters.

The Institute published several proposals aimed at redressing this imbalance. It first broached the subject with *Town and Country Chaos*, by Robert Jones, who later entered Parliament and became an Environment minister. Rob studied the US city of Houston, Texas, where instead of zoning laws (planning controls), the city made extensive use of restrictive covenants. Very broadly there was a presumption in favour of development, but with covenants attached to many properties controlling the type of development that might take place. It was suggested that this approach might be tried in the UK.

In a subsequent report, *The Green Quadratic*, we pointed out that current residents had nothing to gain by supporting development. They lost some amenity and received nothing in return. Similarly business development did not bring much benefit to the local authority where central government received the taxes it paid.

The paper proposed that in some cases of proposed development there could be a local vote to accept or reject a cash sum offered to those affected. The idea was to give communities some stake in development

The ASI's most radical proposal in this field came with *Land Economy* by Mischa Balen. This proposed converting parts of the green belt from monoculture fields of cash crops into woodland surrounding new communities. The suggestion was that great prairies of wheat or rapeseed are not particularly environmentally attractive as diverse habitats and woodland might represent an improvement. The ratio suggested was that 90 per cent of each 100 acres developed should be wooded (including small lakes and rivers), with 5 per cent for housing and 5 per cent for supporting infrastructure.

The proposal was that prime farmland around cities might be converted in such a fashion. The report showed that converting 3 per cent of farms to housing and woodland in England and Wales over a ten-year period would create 950,000 new houses and almost 130,000 hectares of woodland. It would represent 'a regreening of England', as the report put it, increasing its woodland cover by 11 per cent. What it offered to existing country dwellers was the replacement of somewhat unfriendly and unsightly crop fields by woods that would provide a habitat for birds, small mammals and insects. Crucially, none of the new communities established in this way would be overlooked by existing country residents.

The report provoked much conversation in the media, with lively radio discussions and phone-ins. Most people praised its innovative approach, though the organizations claiming to represent country life and values opposed it because it would mean more development, and they opposed all development outside of existing cities.

It did provide a classic illustration of our 'public choice' approach. When one group enjoys a special benefit that excludes others, conventional politics comes down to a test of strength to see which group has the power to thwart the other, and people fight more determinedly to preserve a benefit they have than others will fight to gain one they do not have. Those with the benefit are self-aware and better organized in consequence. The Institute's approach is not to confiscate that benefit, but to trade it, if possible, so those who give it up will gain something of equal or greater vale in return.

In the case of planning controls, those who might lobby to prevent any development might agree to one that improves their own immediate environment. *Land Economy* gained support from some environmentalists who deplored the spread of prairie-type agriculture with its use of fertilizers and pesticides, and welcomed the chance to replace it by natural woodland. Some were prepared to concede the extra housing as part of the price to obtain that.

27

EXILE AND MEZZANINE

The Adam Smith Institute enjoyed a good relationship over the years with Church House, the landlords of its offices. There were two occasions when we had to move out and ship the Institute elsewhere while work was done on the building in Great Smith Street.

One summer while they were working on our office we were offered an office deeper inside Church House. It had the difficulty that it was quite hard to find within Church House unless we tied a ball of twine like Theseus in the Labyrinth. We solved that by putting up direction signs. Our temporary office did have the huge advantage of being quiet, light and airy, and with a view that looked out onto the green behind Westminster Abbey. Since it was over a summer, when Parliament is not sitting and policy activity moves at a slower pace, we were able to cope quite well.

It was we who had instigated the work on our office. All the time we were in the Smith Street offices, we had never had anywhere of our own in which we could hold meetings, except for the open plan office itself. This was just about OK for the occasional evening meeting, but involved moving all the furniture every time and blocking the desks with bookcases to leave free space in the middle.

We asked Church House if we could install a mezzanine floor to create a boardroom in our very high-ceilinged office. There was much negotiation and meetings with architects, and finally there was agreement. A mezzanine room would be built with a circular metal staircase leading up to it and we would share the costs with Church House.

We invited our supporters to help us meet the costs, and arranged for a roll of honour to adorn the wall of the new room after it was completed. When we saw it we were amazed at the luxury of space it gave us. It was a fine room with a great semi-circular window looking across Great Smith Street to the Department for Education – within spitting distance, as Eamonn put it.

The one drawback was the mass of pipes up against the ceiling of one wall. They were quite an eyesore, but we solved it by putting a huge curved hardboard panel stretching the full width of the room to cover them. On this panel we pasted a giant reproduction of the black and white engraving of St Andrews as it was in 1693. We christened the room 'the St Andrews Room' and adorned it with as many prints of Adam Smith as we could locate.

The room was decidedly cosy and it did not take us long to put it to use. We furnished it with IKEA tables and chairs so it could seat fourteen for lunch in comfort, and sixteen at a pinch. The format we decided on was to have a principal guest for lunch, who would start the talk with a ten-minute introduction. A prominent hourglass, which Eamonn sourced over the internet from a ship's chandler in New England, sat in the middle of the table and kept this to time. We would invite guests with some interest in the principal guest's area of expertise. If it were one of the heads of a regulatory commission, we would invite people with some connection to or interest in the industry involved. Following the introduction, discussion followed with Chatham House rules, under which no one could be quoted by name.

There was only one breach of this, with Digby Jones, former CBI chairman who had come in as a trade minister. He started talking as soon as he came in, before any Chatham House warning could be given. He told us frankly that he didn't want to be corrupted by government or the prospect of a ministerial career – as most MPs would be – and would only be doing the job for eighteen months. One of our guests leaked this to the papers with the spin that he had no confidence in Brown's shambling government and was getting out as fast as possible.

When the story was repeated everywhere, he phoned up and spoke to Eamonn about it. They both agreed that politics was a very dirty business, and continued on good terms.

We called these 'Power Lunches' and the name proved quite a good marketing device, lending them a mystique that added to their attraction. Catering was simple, in that we provided sandwiches, fruit and wine. We had good quality sandwiches brought in and learned quite quickly from watching which ones were first to disappear.

The wheat-free sushi provided to suit my diet proved so popular that we added more of it, so sandwiches and sushi became the order of the day at our Power Lunches. The lunches proved invaluable at keeping us abreast of developments, and able to tune our policy proposals to address directly the problems that departments had identified.

The other major advantage of the Power Lunches was that it enabled us to bring some of our donors in on the action by inviting one or two of them to join us occasionally. It gave them an opportunity to see the Institute in action, indeed, in quite a good light because the discussions were often very frank in addressing the problems of the day, and it made our contributors feel they were part of the action.

It helped with our media relations, too, in that we often invited the editors of various newspaper departments to join us when our principal guest was someone relevant to their area. And one by one we invited the editors of major newspapers to be the principal guest themselves, and we invited other guests we knew would include some they might want to run features about or commission articles from.

The other major use of our St Andrews room was to receive university delegations. Quite often a lecturer from a British or US university would organize a few London meetings for their students, and the Adam Smith Institute would feature among their requests. I do not think we ever refused one. Students would descend on our office, perhaps a couple of dozen at a time, and we could just about squeeze them into our mezzanine room, with some on chairs and some on the floor in front of them. It made quite an intimate lecture room, where previously we had been obliged to book a larger room in Church House next door.

They usually wanted to hear about how the Institute worked, what motivated us and what projects we were currently working on, and we were happy to oblige. Most of the delegations were of students studying economics or political science.

TUFTON STREET

More serious renovation in Church House later on put us out for over a year. They wanted to develop their own conference facilities, and this involved cutting off power and water to our office. More to the point, there was to be constant noise with workmen needing access. Church House agreed to provide us with equivalent accommodation for the year it would take.

We looked at several of the alternative accommodations they offered us and finally chose the one above the ecclesiastical outfitters round the corner in Tufton Street, and one floor above the offices of the Social Market Foundation. It was high up, but gave us more space than we were used to.

There was a boardroom in which we could hold Power Lunches and if we kept open the dividing doors that separated it from another office, there was just about room for us to hold our monthly evening receptions for The Next Generation.

It was something of a cram to fit all our young staff into one office, as they were used to, but we just about managed. As before, Eamonn and I continued to work from the flat in Little Smith Street, just a few paces away.

We were mightily relieved when we could all move back into our offices in Great Smith Street, even if there was that Marie Celeste moment when we found everything was exactly as we had left it a year ago. However, the experience of the extra space at Tufton Street had decided us against holding any meetings other than Power Lunches in our offices. Basically the staff were fed up with the dislocation involved in moving desks, chairs and bookcases around every time.

One of our number was a member of St Stephen's Club, so we began using its rooms for our meetings. It was more expensive, but well worth it for the better location, including the use of their garden on warm summer evenings. We tried holding some of The Next Generation meetings in Westminster pubs, but most of them had quite shabby rooms, and the wine was not as good as our members had been used to, so eventually I transferred the meetings to St Stephen's Club as well.

28

REORGANIZATION

It was the experience of moving out for a year that caused us to take a good look at the ASI and to think about what it might do next. We had little doubt that the Labour government would go its full term until May 2010 and would not be re-elected. It was tired, a visible failure, and Gordon Brown was neither a credible nor popular Prime Minister. The bully-boy tactics and the big clunking fist might have worked for a time to keep him in power with his party, but it was not going to do it with the country.

We assumed this meant a new Conservative administration with fresh faces looking for new ideas. Obviously they would have their own agenda, but it already incorporated some of our thinking and we were confident of our ability to contribute more to it. When governments face problems they are receptive to solutions, especially innovative ones that enable them to go at problems in a different way.

The ASI began to prepare for a change of government. We decided, after a mere thirty years, to go for a more stable approach to staff. Instead of having two directors supported by gap-year kids, recent graduates and interns, and with everyone doing everything, we now decided to specialize. The staff would still be young, but now we'd have them concentrate on one particular job and try to retain them on a long-term basis.

In effect the Institute decided to grow up a little. First off we needed an executive director who would be responsible for day-to-day administration as well as taking part in strategic decisions. One good thing came out of the demise of the Globalization Institute and that was that Tom Clougherty parachuted in to the Adam Smith Institute. We had known him since he first appeared as a student at Freedom Week in Cambridge, and then when we had given the Globalization Institute the use of a spare office while we were in Tufton Street. Tom became our executive director.

We appointed Philip Salter, also in his mid-twenties, as our events director to organize TNG receptions, ISOS meetings, evening seminars and Power Lunches. Sally Thompson became our communications director in charge of press, publicity and our various outreach programmes. Finally Sam Bowman joined us as research director, turning down a much better-paid post in the City because he thought the ASI would be more fun to work for. Sam was keen to meet the Tom Bowman who occasionally wrote on our blog, wondering if they might be related. He was slightly disappointed to learn that 'Tom Bowman' was fictitious, a name we used for posts we did not want to go out under our own names.

We began to put all of our activities onto a regular basis. What had been spasmodic now became systematic. The newsletter which we had sent out to our supporters a few times a year was now turned into an electronic bulletin which Eamonn sent out fort-nightly, and which he contrived to make both chatty and witty. The Power Lunches were now stacked into a programme so that they took place regularly throughout the parliamentary season.

The same was done to our evening seminars. We also started to invite speakers to these events with a longer lead time, sometimes many weeks away, instead of the last-minute scramble that had been our previous practice.

The publications were more difficult to slot into any regular programme because our authors tended to be less than predictable about when their copy would be delivered, but we did our best to ensure that a steady stream of reports would be forthcoming. The publicity for these tended to be somewhat last-minute because we were always anxious to get them out and into the public domain where they could be talked about.

We even put our hopelessly inadequate fund-raising onto a more secure and professional basis. Tim Evans, whom we had known since his student days twenty years earlier, was very good at this, so we brought him in part time as our development officer to ensure that we went about securing support in a more streamlined way than our previous haphazard approach. He managed to attract sponsorship support to many of our activities, especially the ones which involved young people.

The Institute was well on the way to becoming ready to work with a new administration, so we discussed what our priorities would be. Top of the list would be tax reform to stimulate economic growth. The financial crisis that had gripped the world gave this a high priority. The next government looked set to plug the gap by a combination of spending cuts and increased taxes. We were happy with the idea of cutting unnecessary and wasteful programmes, but we knew that tax increases were the wrong approach. The better alternative would be to go for growth with reduced tax rates. We started to plan a series of publications and seminars to hammer this point home.

The second priority was schooling. The next government

had to establish the principle that parents could take their state funding for their child to a school outside the state system. The Conservatives were committed to allow 'free schools' to be established to do this, but had held back on allowing the new ones to be profit-making. We knew that only private capital coming in could create the number of schools required to change the system, as the for-profit schools had done in Sweden. We decided to work to have this change added to the policy.

The third measure we decided to work towards was the establishment of an internal market in health care. That had been started with the budget-holding GPs, then stopped for ideological reasons by Labour's Frank Dobson. We decided to work for the idea to be reintroduced, perhaps under another name, and to make it reach wider than it had done the first time.

In each of these areas we would be retreading ground we had already visited several times, but thought it worthwhile to reassert some of the arguments and evidence, given the prospect of a more receptive administration. The strategy of developing and reiterating an idea through a series of publications and conferences was one we had used many times before, and was entirely consistent with our approach.

COALITION

The result of the 2010 general election took us by surprise, as it did most people. We had reckoned on a small overall Conservative majority, and were somewhat dismayed when it fell short of that. For a few awful days there seemed to be the incredible prospect that the government might remain in office, despite being one of the least successful and least competent governments of modern time. To the ASI this was almost too awful to contemplate.

Then there was the possibility of a minority government with no majority to undertake the major reforms we were convinced Britain needed. The thought of a government that limped along doing only the lowest common denominator things it could put through the House was not an attractive one and did not promise to be a successful one for Britain. At best it might struggle along for a few months before calling a fresh election that might bring a majority government.

Even when the coalition was announced between the Conservatives and Liberal Democrats, there was cause for pessimism at first. It looked very much as though they would implement only such policies as both could agree upon, which were not many in number, and which would have avoided the most pressing problems the nation faced.

Then we saw the coalition document. The ASI called a staff meeting to go over it, and rapidly concluded that this might well be a government we could work with. Instead of the weak things both could agree upon, the two parties seemed to have committed themselves to a bold programme of major reforms, addressing all of the key problem areas.

We took particular pleasure in the declared aim to raise the income tax threshold to £10,000. This was not quite the £12,500 we had been publicly advocating on our website, but it was much higher than the current level, and it had come from the Liberal Democrats, not from the Tories. We liked the commitment to reform in education and health, and saw opportunities to make our own contribution to that process.

There was one thing we could obviously not support. The agreement to raise capital gains tax to be on a par with income tax was economic nonsense and completely ignored the differences between the two. Capital investment was the driving force of growth. To raise capital gains tax to 50 per cent, the top rate of income tax, would have been a disaster, so we decided to make a campaign against that our first priority.

With the exception of that one glaring error, we saw the coalition as something that might achieve things for Britain. At the Institute we decided to see how far we could go by combining Conservative policy on economic matters with Liberal Democrat policy on the civil liberties issues. The only question for the ASI now was to work out the best way of trying to nudge the new government gently but firmly toward a more free-market and libertarian position than it might otherwise have taken.

We were still working out how best to go about this when the phone rang.

INDEX